Jan 0

To Dan Gordon

Good Luck

Jayson C. Pratt

1/14/03

To Van Gordon

Good Luck

Gipper Bill York

LUCKY SHOT

Favorite Hunting Stories of an Arizona Sportsman

Written by
Layne A. Brandt

Copyright © 2002 by Layne A. Brandt

All rights reserved. No part of this book shall be reproduced or transmitted in any form or by any means, electronic, mechanical, magnetic, photographic including photocopying, recording or by any information storage and retrieval system, without prior written permission of the publisher. No patent liability is assumed with respect to the use of the information contained herein. Although every precaution has been taken in the preparation of this book, the publisher and author assume no responsibility for errors or omissions. Neither is any liability assumed for damages resulting from the use of the information contained herein.

ISBN 0-7414-1327-2

Front Cover

Painting by Artist Kathy Bingaman, Green Valley, AZ
Author packing out 50th mountain lion on River with strike dog, Pepper, in the mountains of Southern Arizona. Lion was shot by Darrell Day of Sahuarita, AZ.

Back Cover

"Flyin' Lion" caught by Blackie, Liza, Major, Radar, and Bell Tumacacori Mountains, Southern Arizona, May of 2001. Photo by Carmen Miller
Shot by Mark Helling.

Published by:

519 West Lancaster Avenue
Haverford, PA 19041-1413
Info@buybooksontheweb.com
www.buybooksontheweb.com
Toll-free (877) BUY BOOK
Local Phone (610) 520-2500
Fax (610) 519-0261

Printed in the United States of America

Printed on Recycled Paper

Published December 2002

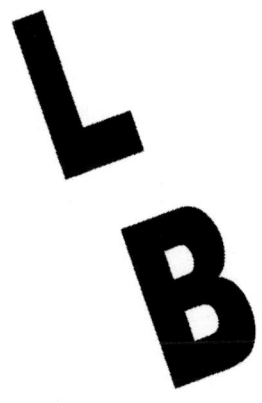

Dedication

I dedicate this book to my loving family: my wife, Eileen; daughters Kelly, Tamara, Lisa and Julie; and son, Allen.

Thank you for putting up with my hunting for all these years. I love you all very much.

A special thanks to Vanessa Lopez, Cynthia Ochoa, and Sandy Parker for all of their help with typing, editing, and expert advice.

Thanks also to all my friends who contributed a great story or photo for this book. I appreciate it.

Preface

My children have told me for years that I should write a book. They grew up listening to hunting stories. I finally decided to put together some of my favorite stories, along with some photographs.

I thank God for being born in a free country, for a loving mother and father, and for the many mentors that have helped shape my life: Ollie Barney, a friend and lion hunting partner; Keith Walden, founder of Farmers Investment Company, who taught me the A-Z's of the farming business; Ken Ethridge, my friend and ranching partner who taught me the ranching business; George Parker, a friend and a world renowned international hunter; and Harlon Carter, a friend and a leader for the NRA and 2nd Amendment Rights.

I hope you enjoy reading this book as much as I have enjoyed writing it.

Layne A. Brandt

"A strong body makes the mind strong. As to the species of exercises, I advise the gun. While this gives moderate exercise to the body, it gives boldness, enterprise and independence to the mind. Games played with the ball, and others of that nature, are too violent for the body and stamp no character on the mind. Let your gun therefore be the constant companion of your walks."

Thomas Jefferson

Foreword

I feel fortunate that I grew up with a father who shared his love of the outdoors with his family. I recall camping trips into the Rocky Mountain region, across the Southwest and even down to Sonora, Mexico, where my sisters and I would watch the road from the camper's overhang above the cab of the pickup. Often, Dad would suddenly see a side road that looked interesting. Our big blue Ford (we named it "Thunder") would lurch onto that side road and the rest of us just hung on and hoped that Dad knew where he was going. We saw a lot of interesting (and rough!) country that way, and we all lived to tell about it (even the time we thought we were goners when getting lost in the middle of the desert in Baja, California), so I suppose I shouldn't complain too loudly. Panoramic mountain ranges, lava beds, deep night skies where all of the stars came out, the desert in bloom, sandy Mexican beaches and body surfing in bathwater-warm waves, long stretches of straight highway that shimmered in the heat of a scorching summer afternoon, scanning the roadside for wildlife ("The first one to see an antelope gets a quarter!"), the snowy roads of Mount Lemon, the grassy plains of Wyoming, the ghost towns of Arizona: these trips taught me to appreciate the beauty of the outdoors.

A few memories stand out in particular. One is probably more a memory of my parents talking about it rather than the actual events: We were at the beach in Mexico, probably near Guaymas or Rocky Point, and at four or five years of age, I was standing in the surf with a fishing pole about twice my height. Somehow I hooked a fish and started reeling it in, but it was very strong and put up quite a fight. Apparently I slung the fishing pole up onto my shoulder, turned around and started marching up that beach – and dragged the fish right out of the water. That big flounder ended up buried in a barbeque pit on that same beach, not too bad of a job for such a young 'un.

Another memory is bird hunting with Dad, which was a lot of fun for me as a young girl. We'd wake up at oh-dark-thirty and drive out near the pecan groves where we'd crouch among huge brush piles and mounds of empty pecan husks and broken shells. I'd be wearing a hunting vest with side pockets stuffed with extra shells, and was usually carrying a .410/.22 over and under as I kneeled on the ground, scanning the skies for mourning doves. I liked spotting Gambel's quail, which were much easier to shoot as they scurried across the ground. Sometimes we had a bird dog with us, and sometimes it was me who played retriever (I also got to open and close a lot of gates). The smell of gunpowder always makes me think of those Saturday morning bird hunts.

Now, I look at children who are growing up in big cities and hope that someone is showing them the beauty and enjoyment that can be found in the country. Especially in today's busy society, people need to slow down once in a while, get out of town where it's peaceful and quiet, recharge their batteries and enjoy the outdoors. What's important in life is more evident once you've gained a little perspective by getting away from it all for a while – I highly recommend it.

Kelly (Brandt) Haskins

Troutdale, Oregon

June 2002

Kelly Brandt (age 7) with pet coyote.

Contents

The Hunter 1
Dad's Advice 3
Political Advice 5
Harlon Carter's Texas Deer Hunt 5
Expert Advice 7
Doctors and Pheasant Hunting Season 9
First Pheasant 10
My First Lion Hunt 12
My Second Lion Hunt 14
Lion Fever 17
Lucky Bowhunter 20
Box Canyon Lion 22
The Perils of Lion Hunting 24
The Making of a Lion Dog 25
Lion Hunter Humor 29
Short Stories 33
Jeep Wreck 39
Cowboy Humor 41
1921-2001 44
Del Goodin's Lion Stories 45
Record Book Cheetah 48
Safari 2001 - Around the World in 55 Days 50

Mexico Dove Hunt	80
Nevada Lion Hunt	81
Mexico Turkeys I	83
Mexico Turkeys II	86
Mexican Lion Hunt	87
Lucky Pilot	90
Two Lions Off One Kill	91
Lion Hunter	97
White Mountain Turkeys	100
Arizona Black Bear Hunt	103
The Lee Brothers	104
A Covey of Lions	106
Alaska Grizzly Bear	111
Fly In Fishing	113
New Mexico Stories	117
Lori's Buck	131
Sonora, Mexico Coues Deer Hunt	132
The Successful Lion Hunt	136
Muy Grande!	139
The One of a Kind Trophy	141
Colorado Elk	145
Tried and True	147

Dr. Green's Virgin Elk Hunt 149

Rena's Lion 154

Record Book Sheep Horns 157

Princess, the Bucking Mule 159

Spilsbury's Hounds 165

'83 Flood 168

Pecan Orchard Attacks Border Patrol 170

Mexico Border Lion 174

Roos and Cockatoos 176

Javelina in a Tree 179

George Parker's Lion 180

Sonoita Creek Lion 185

Pinta's First Puma 187

Two For The Price of One 189

Santa Rita Ranch Calf Killer 191

Picnics and Pumas 193

Old Hunting Dog 195

Lucky Wetback 197

Big Moose – Big Lion 198

The NRA and ILA 203

The Hunter

Beryl J. Barney

Hunting is the sport of special men,
Whose love for hunting is an inborn thing
Inherited through many generations,
Down through the ages from prehistoric man
Who hunted for survival of his clan.

A hunter loves the forests and the hills,
The deserts and the mountains where
Afoot or horseback, he may find a trail
To follow elk or bear or ram,
Or mountain lion, tracking with his hounds.

A hunter loves the challenge of the stalk –
Whether the animal is smarter than the man.
All animals are beautiful to him
And, caring thus, he seeks the older ones
To grace his trophy room or make the book.

A hunter understands the constant need
For habitat, and food enough for all.
He knows that winter often takes its toll
When snow is deep and food is scarce,
That some will starve and some will die of cold.

The same in summer drought when streams are low
Water holes dry up and the weak ones die.
The hunter, then, is conservationist.
By hunting older lion, buck, or ram
He leaves the young to carry species on,

That coming generations might enjoy
This oldest sport of man and prove their skill
At shooting clean and true with bow or gun.
Learning the lessons those before them knew,
They find that hunting is much more than fun.

Dad's Advice

I guess the seed didn't fall very far from the tree when I was born. My dad was an avid hunter, as was his dad. So I suppose it was only natural that hunting was my choice of sports.

Dad used to say, "Son, every man needs a hobby. Don't wait until you retire. That's too late. You need to start young and enjoy your hobby all of your life. If you work hard and play hard and be honest in all of your dealings, you will lead a happy and productive life." I have always tried to follow my dad's advice.

Dad passed away in 1998. He was my friend, a hunting companion, and a world-class father. My family and I will miss him always.

My mother passed away in 2001. She was a wonderful wife, mother, grandmother, and great grandmother. My family and I miss her very much.

Otto Brandt   Sophia Brandt

1923-1998   1923-2001

Photo taken at Otto and Sophia Brandt's
50th wedding anniversary in 1993.

The Brandt Family

Left to right: Tamara Brandt, Julie (Brandt) Rayner, Eileen Brandt, Allen Brandt (front), Layne Brandt (rear), Lisa Brandt, Dan Haskins, Kelly (Brandt) Haskins, Sophia Brandt, and Otto Brandt.

Tucson, Arizona 1993

Political Advice

I became good friends with Harlon Carter after he retired from running the NRA for many years.

One day I called Harlon and I invited him over to shoot a few ravens. I was having difficulty making up my mind about how to vote in an upcoming election between two candidates. I liked one of the candidates very well, but with one exception. The exception was that he was not a very strong gun advocate. When I explained my dilemma to Harlon he said, "Layne, the answer is simple. If a man doesn't think right about guns you can't expect him to think right about anything else!"

Ollie's dad once told him he only voted for a Democrat once. "He was a horse thief, and I voted to hang him!" He explained.

The NRA does a good job, in my opinion, of checking out perspective political candidates. They also notify members of their recommendations. I rarely vote contrary to NRA recommendations. I am a single-issue voter. I vote for the candidate that, in my opinion, is the strongest supporter of gun rights and personal freedom.

Harlon Carter's Texas Deer Hunt

I named this book after Harlon Carter's Texas deer hunting story. Harlon said that he and his dad were hunting Whitetail Deer in the brush country of South Texas. They were walking along a fence line when all of a sudden, out of the brush, ran a big Whitetail buck. Harlon's dad raised up his rifle to shoot. At the same instant, the buck jumped the fence. Harlon's dad shot when the buck was in mid-air. The buck fell dead on the other side. Harlon was very young at the time and had never seen anything like that. "Wow, Dad, what a lucky shot!" His dad turned to Harlon and said, "What do you mean lucky? I was shooting at him, wasn't I?"

And so, in remembrance of the late Harlon Carter, a dear friend of mine, I'm titling this book in honor of him.

Harlon B. Carter
1913-1991

Expert Advice

When I became acquainted with George Parker he was about 70 years old. He was a very well-known hunter all over the world. I was very fascinated by his trophy room and his hunting stories. When he became ill with cancer, he would call me up about once a week and he would say, "Layne, stop by the house for a drink." George and I would visit, and I never would get tired of his stories of hunting around the world. Occasionally Col. Charlie Askins would visit and the 3 of us would go raven hunting or quail hunting on the Farm. I always liked Charlie - a good guy and a hell of a good shot. His book, "Unrepentant Sinner" is one of my favorites.

George always told me if I met someone I wanted to get better acquainted with that I should go hunting with them. He said, "You will either have a friend for life or you will never want to see the S.O.B. again!"

In George Parker's book you were either a good S.O.B. or a no-good S.O.B., there was no "in between". I became very good friends with George. His death left a void in my life that will never be replaced.

One day he called me up with the usual "stop by for a drink." When I got there he said, "Layne, this cancer is about to do me in. I'm not going to be around much longer. I have a favor to ask of you."

I assured him, "George, if it is within my means, it will be done." George told me that he wanted to be cremated and that Ollie Barney knew exactly where his ashes were to be spread. He asked me if I would fly the airplane, along with Ollie, and disperse of his ashes. I told him that I would be honored to do so.

It wasn't long after that day that George died. Soon after, his widow, Jackie, called Ollie and I to set up the time for George's "aerial burial". Ollie and I took care of the burial and soon after that we, Ollie and I, became the best of friends. George had told me that I needed to get better acquainted with Ollie. "He is one hell of a good guy," he said to me.

George's final words of advice to me were:

1. Never be without a gun. This world is dangerous and you never know when you might have to defend yourself and shoot some S.O.B.

2. You need to think about all of the possible situations you may find yourself in one day, then plan exactly what to do. When

you find yourself in a bad situation, don't take valuable time to think, just act and act quickly. It will likely save your life. And, be damned sure he is dead. You don't want two stories in the courtroom, only yours.

3. Never pass up an opportunity to go hunting. You will never be able to make it up. Borrow the money, take time off work, and go. You will never regret it.

I have been very fortunate in my life to have the advice of my father, George Parker, and others.

Dale Lee had some great advice for anyone who shoots a gun. The key to hitting what you are shooting at is to pull the trigger at the right time! If he were alive today, he would probably have a bumper sticker that reads:

"Gun Control is being able to hit what you aim at!"

It's the only form of gun control that I support.

George W. Parker, Jr.
1908-1984

Doctors and Pheasant Hunting Season

One of the first hunting stories I can recall is about my dad. My mother was pregnant with my younger brother, Dale, in 1946. The baby was due to be born on October 12. My mother, for whatever reason, had all three of her children by cesarean section. She and her doctor set the October 12th date and then she informed my dad of the news.

When my mom told my dad, he got up from the kitchen table and walked over to the calendar, which was hanging on the wall. After a few minutes he said, "Sue, you will need to change the date. October 12th is the first day of pheasant season!" The date was changed and Dale was born on October 16, 1946. There was speculation that the doctor was a pheasant hunter also! And, dad got to go hunting on the first day of pheasant season as was the tradition.

Left to Right: Howard Wiersma (Otto Brandt's brother-in-law), Otto Brandt, and Layne Brandt (age 2) Holland, MI 1946

First Pheasant

When I was 10 years old, my parents gave me a .410 shotgun (single shot) and a .22 rifle (single shot). This was a big upgrade from my current .22 Daisy B.B. Gun. My dad had already schooled me on gun safety and I was permitted to hunt on the family farm and on several neighboring farms.

When pheasant season rolled around it was like a national holiday where we lived. The schools might as well have closed. Most of the boys (and many girls) went hunting. Dad always took the day off of work. It was a day to look forward to. I could never sleep well the night before pheasant season because I would be too excited, anticipating the morning hunt.

I didn't get a rooster on the first day of the hunt. I was always with older men, and they could shoot faster than I could; and they also had bigger guns than I had. On the second day of the hunt I had to go to school; however, my parents would let me go hunting before school. On the third or fourth day of the hunting season, there came a light snow. "Great!" I thought, "Tracking snow." I was very excited, and as soon as there was enough light to see what I was hunting I was out in the field. I hadn't gone very far when I cut the fresh track of a pheasant. I figured that it was a rooster because I could see the track where its tail was dragging in the snow. Man, I was excited! I trailed the rooster up when, suddenly, he practically flew up under my feet! I almost dropped my gun! Those roosters really cackle loud. When I finally got my wits about me, the rooster was almost out of range; however, a lucky shot brought him down. I was tickled to death. My first rooster!

I doubt if I did well in school that day. It was a one-room country school with one teacher for 8 grades. My friend, Glenn Vande Vusse, and I were the only two in our fifth grade class. I'm sure he got tired of hearing about my first rooster!

**Layne's Brittany Spaniel with rooster pheasant
1954**

My First Lion Hunt

It was in 1975 when I decided to add a mountain lion to my list of trophies. I did some checking around and found out that Clay Howell from Patagonia had a good reputation and wasn't too far away. I called him up and set up a time to visit. We met at his ranch (Lazy RR) just outside of Patagonia and we had a good visit. I liked Clay from the start. He was a rancher, a hunter, and he was easy going. When I left he said, "When I see some fresh sign or a kill, or something to go on, I'll give you a call."

I told my boss, Dick Walden, that I would need to take my vacation on a moment's notice to make this lion hunt deal work. He said, "No problem. Just call my assistant, Lorrell Clark, and work out the details." Dick and Lorrell were both good guys to work for. I still work for Dick.

One night about dinnertime, the phone rang, and it was Clay. "We had a fresh snow in the mountains. Let's go look for a lion track in the morning." I called Lorrell, and at 3:00 the next morning I was having breakfast at Clay's ranch. We loaded the dogs and horses and trailed to a place in the Patagonia Mountains that Clay wanted to check for tracks. We couldn't find a lion track but we found a bobcat track. Clay asked me if I wanted a bobcat. Even though I had shot a bobcat, I wanted to see the dogs work. They had that bobcat treed in no time. I shot it out with Clay's rifle and we went home. It was a beautiful bobcat with a good coat. It was February and cold.

A few days later Clay called again and said he had been seeing signs of a big male lion, and he wanted to make another hunt. This time we trailed to the south end of the Santa Rita Mountains. We rode up a long ridge; Clay was riding a horse and I was riding a mule. We got pretty high on this ridge and there was a small saddle. Clay's strike dog hit a track and was out of hearing in no time. We had 4 young dogs with us, and they were necked together in pairs behind my mule. Clay flew off his horse and hollered at me, "Grab those young dogs and hold them." Now that was a chore. Those dogs wanted to go on that track real bad. They were a handful. Clay went to look for sign to see if his strike dog was going in the right direction before turning the young dogs loose. Clay found a lion scratch and the strike dog was going right. He unleashed the 4 young dogs, and the race was on. We rode as far as we could. When it got too steep, we tied up our mounts and went on foot. I was a lot younger than Clay and I still had trouble keeping up. One tough hombre! When we got to the top of the next ridge we could hear the dogs barking treed at the base of a big rock pile. In a minute, I saw the lion moving, and he went over the top and was out of sight. In a few minutes, the dogs picked up the track on the other side of the rock pile and trailed down the canyon. They soon had the lion treed in a big oak tree. It sure was a sight to see my first lion. I shot it out and it was a real nice tom. Clay packed it out on his horse and we made for the ranch. I had a taxidermist make a rug out of the hide. It did not make the Arizona Record Book, but it came real close.

It was then that I decided I wanted to do some lion hunting someday. I have been around dogs and horses all of my life and this looked like a sport I could get into.

After telling some of my hunting buddies about my future plans, they told me to take 2 aspirins and to elevate my feet until the feeling went away!

Author's Note: Clay Howell went to the happy hunting grounds in July of 2001. I attended his funeral, and it was standing room only. Clay was a good hunter, a good guy, a good rancher, and a good guide. He will be missed by many.

Author with first lion, 1975

My Second Lion Hunt

Ten years had elapsed since I got my first lion in 1975. Ollie Barney and I became good friends after George Parker's "aerial burial."

Ollie called one night and said he got a call on a calf killed by a lion. The next morning I met him real early and we made a circle. The dogs trailed the lion up into some bluffs, but it got away from the dogs.

Ollie and I hunted off and on throughout that summer exercising dogs. In September when it started to cool off a little, we made a circle in the north end of the Santa Rita Mountains in the vicinity of Helvetia (mining camp). We were riding down a granite ridge when the dogs (we had 7 dogs) threw their heads up and screamed off the ridge. "This is the track we have been looking for!" exclaimed Ollie. We rode for a long ways to catch up with the dogs. They were trailing slowly, and Ollie "suspicioned" that they were on the wrong end of the track. Soon after, Ollie found the lion track in a sand wash and, sure enough, they were on the back track. We turned the dogs around and started back to where we started the track. Ollie looked around and said, "I don't see Drifter anywhere. Maybe he took the other end of the track." That is exactly what happened. When we got back on top, we could hear Drifter barking treed. When those other hounds heard Drifter, they took off like shot. In a few minutes they were all barking treed. Ollie and I rode as far as we could and then we started walking. They had this lion caught in some big high bluffs. We slipped around in the rocks until I could get a shot. It was a real treat to see this big tom standing on that bluff watching those dogs. After I shot the lion, it fell a long ways. Ollie and I had to work our way off the ridge down to where the lion was. I packed it out on my horse. This lion did make the record book.

On the way home I asked Ollie what I owed him. He said, "I'll take ½ interest in your airplane (company airplane) and you fly it!" We have been good friends ever since.

Ollie has taught me a lot about lion hunting. He and I became partners on a pack of dogs, and we have caught lots of lions together.

Ollie can look at a lion track and tell you how old the lion is, how big it is, the sex, and when it will be back!

I have seen a total of 70 lions in trees or bluffs since 1975. It is a sport that gets in your blood. I call it "lion fever".

I value Ollie's friendship and knowledge. He was 83 in January 2002 and he is still hunting. He has caught about 200 lions in Arizona. He has hunted all over the world, and I never get tired of his stories.

Hounds can be real hard to keep track of when hunting in these rough mountains. Sometimes it takes days to get all your dogs back. Whenever Ollie and I get back with all of our dogs, we consider that "a successful hunt"!

Ollie Barney with Layne's 2nd lion.

"Dos Amigos", Ollie and Layne.
Santa Rita Mountains
1985

Lion Fever

Once Ollie felt I had learned enough about handling hounds and lion hunting, he started letting me borrow a couple dogs now and then to go by myself. It wasn't long before I bought a hound of my own and a pup that Ollie said he would help train.

One thing led to another and I started scouting for an area near my home where I could hunt for a day when I could get away from the pecan farm. I had learned enough from Ollie that I knew I didn't want to hunt in another lion hunter's area without discussing it with them first. I called an old acquaintance, Clay Howell, who has been lion hunting in the Santa Rita Mountains for many years. I explained to him this fever that I had contracted and he was real quick to understand the problem. We met for coffee in Nogales and talked about an area that he was no longer active in, and he said he would be very pleased if I would hunt this area. He also went on to tell me some of the areas in particular that the lions used most frequently. So I started hunting in this area and started finding a little lion sign. After making a lot of horse tracks, I felt I had an area picked out where I could catch a lion.

In April of 1986, I asked an employee of mine, Juan Lopez, if he wanted to go hunting Saturday morning. He had been hunting with me some and really wanted to kill a lion. I had killed one with Clay Howell and Ollie Barney, so I was more interested in catching one than killing one. Well, we had this hunt all lined up but when Saturday morning came I realized I was one horse short. A friend of mine had borrowed one of my horses to work cattle with on Friday and failed to return him as he said he would. So I called Juan and explained my problem to him. Well, anyway, I decided to go ahead and make the hunt "solo" to exercise the dogs. I took two of Ollie's dogs and one of mine. I rode up the trail to this saddle I had named "Lion Saddle" because of the sign I had been seeing there. As soon as I got there, Abe and Sport barked about the same time and took off down this ridge. I jumped off my horse and checked for sign and I saw the scratch of a big Tom, and the dogs were headed in the right direction. This ridge was too rough for my horse, so I tied him up and grabbed my canteen and rifle and took off after the dogs. I could still hear them trailing, but not very fast. All of a sudden I heard Pepper start yipping and running, and I knew they had the lion jumped. They went about a quarter of a mile when they started barking treed. I slipped up there and stayed high on the ridge so I could see what was going on. There was a big Ponderosa pine and those dogs were really excited. I looked and looked, but I couldn't see the lion. I was afraid he had jumped out and got away. I finally saw this big Tom walk out on a limb and just stand there and watch those dogs. I shot him out with my trusty .30-.30.

It was then I realized I was a long way from my horse, and it was getting hot. I sharpened my knife and went to skinning this lion. It was a steep hillside and hard work. After I got him skinned out, I took the last drink out of my canteen and took off for my horse. That horse was sure a welcome sight. After the drying period, I had the lion measured for the record book and have since entered it in the AWF state record book.

I have hunted many species of big game including nine of the Big 10 in Arizona. I have hunted in several of the western states including Alaska, as well as in Mexico. But for my money, I'll take lion hunting with a good pack of hounds over any other hunting I that I have done.

Thanks to the help and support of friends and family, I am able to do enough hunting to keep the fever down and, with Allen now seven years old, I look forward to the day when he can go hunting big game with me. He will be the fourth generation hunter in our family; and, who knows, he might even get a case of lion fever someday himself.

Layne receives the S.C.I. "Fraker Award" from Ollie in 1990 for the story "Lion Fever".

Lucky Bowhunter

One year in August, Ollie Barney, Ray McGee and myself decided to fly up to Northern Arizona for a Sunday, rent a car, and drive around and shoot some prairie dogs. We met at the Continental Airstrip, where F.I.C.O. keeps their airplanes, at 5:00 a.m. We loaded our rifles and ammo into the Cessna 182 and took off. When we got airborne, we could see heavy cloud cover all around. We decided to land in Tucson and have breakfast and check the weather. The weather forecast was not good for VFR flying. We ate breakfast and flew back home. We decided to drive around the desert at home and shoot a few jackrabbits. It started to rain, and we never saw a rabbit or ever fired a shot. It looked like we were not going to hunt anything that day. About noon we all went home, disappointed about the day in general. We were all looking forward to a fun day. It looked like the prairie dogs were going to have a better day than us.

I went home and decided to take a siesta. As luck would have it, I no sooner fell asleep and the phone rang. It was Ray. He got a call from a bow hunter (deer season was open for bow and arrow hunting) who wounded a lion the day before. Ray told the guy we would go have a look around. By then it was raining fairly hard. I told Ray I thought we were wasting our time trying to trail a 24-hour-old track in the rain. He agreed it was a long shot. We loaded 2 horses and 3 dogs and drove about 10 miles to meet the bow hunter. He showed us exactly where this wounded lion had crossed a dirt road.

I was ready to go home. I didn't think the dogs had a chance of trailing this lion, but the bow hunter sure wanted us to try. We turned out one good strike dog we called "Buck". I walked along where this lion went. Buck started to get a little interested. Finally he meandered down into the canyon and let out a bawl. The 2 dogs in the trailer went berserk. We turned them loose and they joined Buck muy pronto. Apparently there was enough blood from the lion to follow the trail. There was only a small spot of blood every 20 or so yards that I could see. Those experienced lion dogs never cease to amaze me.

We told the hunter to listen to the dogs, as to which way they were going. Ray and I drove the truck up the road a mile or so until we found a place to turn around. When we got back and parked the truck, we could hear the dogs barking treed. The hunter asked, "What are those dogs barking at?" I said, "I don't know. They may have found a house cat or something!" Ray said, "Let's go down and have a look. Leave the bow and arrow and bring a rifle. We don't want this lion to get away a 2nd time. Layne and I don't like hunting in the rain!" We went down there and the hunter shot the lion out of a small mesquite tree. It was a nice average size male lion. The hunter was very happy and grateful. Ray and I were amazed at the ability of those hounds. We are sure this lion laid up to lick his wounds. He was only about 300-400 yards from where he was shot the 1st time.

This is the only time I have caught a lion without unloading the horses. We didn't have any luck flying or shooting jackrabbits, but we sure had luck with hunting a wounded lion in the rain.

Ray McGee with male lion
Shot by Matt Smith of Phoenix, AZ

Box Canyon Lion

Seven o'clock that morning my cell phone rang. It was Joe Robinson, a local rancher and a friend of mine. He said that he had found a place for me to hunt that Sunday. "Why's that Joe?" I asked.

"I just saw a fresh lion track," he answered.

"You didn't find a place for me to hunt Sunday; you found a place for me to hunt today!" I exclaimed, "That lion might be 200 miles from here by Sunday." (I think this was on Thursday when I talked to Joe.)

I called Juanito Lopez, a 20-year-old friend of mine who wanted a lion. "Meet me at Joe's place, muy pronto! I'll be there as soon as I can load the dogs and the horses."

We met at the ranch where Joe was waiting for us. Joe and I walked up the canyon a short ways so that he could show me the tracks. The dogs took it right away and trailed up to a dam. There were some cattle around the dam and they stomped out the lion scent. I made a circle on foot and found where the lion went up a side canyon. I called the hounds and they took the track. I walked back to the ranch to get my horse, and then Juanito and I headed for the dogs. Joe had other business to tend to. But he had already done his part. As Warner Glenn would say, "My telephone is my best strike dog."

Those hounds hammered on that track from 8:00 until 11:30 am. It was a hot August day. They had hell trailing. We heard them when they jumped the lion. They had it bayed on a big rock. Juanito made a good shot. It was a big record book tom.

It was then that I noticed "Kelly" limping. On this hunt I had three of Brian Thomas' dogs and two of mine and Ollie's dogs. Brian is a real good lion hunter and is also a friend of mine from Northern Arizona. He and Chuck Lange have helped me train some pups, and they have also loaned me dogs on occasion. They are both good friends, good hunters, and good dog trainers.

I picked Kelly up and packed her out on my horse. Juanito walked and packed the lion out on his mare.

Joe Robinson is also a vet. I had him check Kelly's leg. He said it was a slight fracture and not to hunt her for awhile. With a lot of tender loving care and a hot dog a day, she fully recovered from her injury.

Joe was sure glad we caught this big tom before he started killing calves.

Juanito with record book male lion on Brownie.

Dogs listed from front to rear: Major, Bell, Blackie, Liza and Kelly

The Perils of Lion Hunting

Lion hunting with hounds in the rugged mountains of Southern Arizona has always had its perils...lions killing dogs, dogs getting knocked off bluffs, snake bites, bears, javelina, coati mundis, poison bait, heat stroke, getting hit by a car, getting shot mistakenly by a client, or people stealing dogs. It's a small wonder a man can keep a pack of dogs. At $2,000-$5,000 a lion, the clients get a real bargain.

I have also heard of dogs falling into abandoned mine shafts and the list goes on. The most recent incident I have heard of is dogs getting killed by Africanized killer bees. I have even heard of a case where a lion drowned a dog in a small creek.

Now the Game Department has re-introduced Mexican wolves in Northern Arizona. I'm told the wolves hear the dogs barking and will investigate what's going on. If a dog gets into a fight with a wolf a dog could get killed real easy. The Game Department wants lion hunters to pull their dogs off a jaguar track and not let the dogs trail it. Most of the time I don't see _any_ tracks in the rock piles I'm hunting in! If I ever mistakenly catch a jaguar, I plan to take a picture of it and turn it loose.

I'm concerned that the State of Arizona will follow suit with California, Oregon and Washington where it is illegal to hunt lions with hounds. If, or when, that happens I may move to Africa.

The Making of a Lion Dog

By Blackie Barney Brandt

I was born in May of 1995 in Layne's dog pen. My mother's name was Sally and my dad's name was Ike. Mother is a cross-bred hound and my dad is ½ cross-bred hound and ½ Catahoula. Layne and Ollie and their predecessors have been breeding the best to the best for over 100 years. So, my chances of becoming a well-trained lion dog some day were pretty good.

I had 7 brothers and sisters when I was born. Layne and Ollie gave them all away, except me! Am I lucky or what! I think they liked me because I am solid coal black – not a white or brown hair on my body. My toenails and eyes are black. I think I'm pretty good lookin'.

When I was weaned at 6 weeks old, Layne and Ollie gave away all my brothers and sisters. Man, was I lonesome. I cried day and night.

When I was about 6 months old, Layne and Ollie started taking me along on lion hunts. What a great sport! I enjoyed chasing deer and coyotes, but Layne and Ollie were not happy about that. I eventually quit that. I still have fond memories of chasing my first deer. They smell good!

When I was about a year old, Layne sent me to his good friend and ranching partner, Chuck Lange, to do some hunting up north in the Wickenburg, Kingman area. Chuck treated me real good. I liked him. Pretty good at ridin' buckin' horses, too! Chuck and his dogs taught me a lot about lion huntin'. One day I overheard Chuck talking to Layne on the phone. He told Layne he didn't know if I would make a lion dog or not. I was heartbroken. I made up my mind I would show him!!

The next time we went lion huntin', I found the lion all by myself. I'll show him what I'm made of! I ran the lion down the ridge and bayed her on the ground by myself! Chuck and the other dogs were proud of me! I missed Layne and Ollie and hoped to go home soon.

Layne must have read my mind. He showed up one day soon after and I thought they would never stop talking. I think they need to talk less and hunt more!

I was only home for a short time when Ollie came and picked me up. Lion huntin' time! It was good to see my mom and dad and some of the other dogs. Good friends, lots of fun.

Ollie had a friend by the name of George Brown. Nice guy. We went hunting at the McGee Ranch not far from home. We stayed at Ray McGee's house.

The first morning we went hunting. We started down a big long deep canyon that runs off to the south. We didn't go very far until I found a fresh lion track. The other dogs found another track and trailed down the canyon. The one I found went up. I only went a little ways when I found this lion! I chased him up a tree and barked at him as loud as I could. Where are George and Ollie? I'll bet they went to follow them other dogs. Oh, here they come! I hope this lion doesn't jump out. Dang, there he goes! I'm going to make that lion go back up the same tree! I want Ollie to be proud of me. The lion put up quite a fuss, but he finally went back up that same tree. George made a good shot. I knew he would. Ollie and George are proud of me! I know Layne will be, too.

One day Ray McGee found a fresh deer killed by a lion. He called Layne to tell him the news. Layne had to work (that guy works too much) the next day. He helped Ray with a hunter and some dogs. I was one of the lucky ones! Yea! Jim Bickle drove down from Phoenix to go on this hunt. Layne, Ollie and Ray had donated a lion hunt to raise money for some good cause. I don't remember what for. Ollie and Layne and Ray have donated several hunts; Ollie more than Layne and Ray. Good guys. Anyway, Ray picked me up and took me to his house where Jim Bickle was waiting.

Early the next morning we rode up to the kill. The other dogs and me took off. Fresh track…just the kind I like. In no time we had 2 lions caught! One of the cowboys shot the 1st one. All of the dogs left me and went to the kill. I decided to stay and keep this other lion treed for Jim Bickle. I don't like to see these lions get away. Ray and Jim rode up in a little while and Jim made a good shot. Pretty nice lion! Big male! Ray and Jim were proud.

In the country we hunt in, there are quite a few chulas (coati mundis). I like to catch one once in a while, but I'm thinking about quitting. I had one tear a hole in my neck and Ollie and Buck Garner had to rush me to the hospital. Ollie stuffed some cloth in my neck to slow down the bleeding. Simon Escalada put in over 100 stitches! I'll probably live a long time if I leave those mean bastards alone. I know Layne and Ollie want me to quit. I'm still thinking about it.

So far I have helped Layne and Ollie and Ray and Chuck catch over 40 lions. I hope to catch a lot more. It's a great sport for those of us lucky enough to learn how. Some dogs never learn.

I still live in the dog pen where I was born. I overheard Ollie and Layne talking one day. They said they would never sell me. They said I would get killed lion hunting or die in the dog pen. I promise I'll be careful! I love you guys!

Author's granddaughters, Jackie and Lauren Rayner, with Blackie Barney Brandt.

George Brown

Lion Hunter Humor

By Ollie Barney

These are 5 short stories that kind of indicate that some lion hunters have got a sense of humor.

Dale Lee

The first one is about Dale Lee. He was camped down in Sawmill Canyon in the Santa Rita's and these two other lion hunters rode into his camp along in the afternoon. Dale was already in camp. They visited awhile, sitting on their horses. Dale then said to them, "Well, get down. I've got some coffee here."

Dale was camped there in a tent. They got down and Dale poured them both a cup of coffee. This one feller says, "Dale, don't you have any sugar?" Dale says, "Yes, I've got sugar."

He went in his tent and came out with an unopened 5-pound sack of sugar. Dale tore the corner off of it, and the guy stuck his cup out. And, old Dale poured in about a half cup of sugar and ran out about half of his coffee! He says, "You want sugar - there's sugar!" He turned around and took his sugar back in the tent. He came back and went on a-visitin'. Dale never cracked a smile or said anything about the sugar. This guy set his half cup of sugar and coffee down and never said anything to Dale about it.

Lloyd Smith

This is a story that Lloyd Smith told me on himself. He was hunting over in New Mexico with a mutual friend of ours. He was a cowboy over there and was hunting out of his cow camp. Lloyd said that it was getting up in the spring of the year, fairly warm, and they had hunted and gotten back about 2:00 p.m. They hadn't had any lunch, hadn't had a drink of water or anything. They went into the kitchen of this cow camp, opened the refrigerator and got two cans of Coors out. He set the one down there at his place at the table and set the other can of Coors over in front of Lloyd.

Lloyd said, "Don't you have anything but scab beer?" This guy says, "No", and just reached over, picked up the can of beer and set it back in the icebox. And Lloyd said, "I went without beer, but sure wish I would have kept my mouth shut! That beer would have tasted good."

Ted Fergason

This story is on Sewell Goodman and Ted Fergason. Ted is dead now, but he was a lion hunter that used to hunt out of Safford. He had farmed all over there and made quite a little money. He retired, and that's all he did was lion hunting. If any of the ranches around had a lion problem, they called Ted up, and he would go out and hunt.

Sewell used to hunt with him a lot. Ted was real frugal, but he always had lots of groceries in his camp. He ate well. So they say. I never did hunt with him.

One morning there, Sewell likes a little sugar in his coffee. He gets his teaspoon and sees that Ted is watching him. Ted didn't use sugar in his coffee.

It was a luxury. Sewell puts three big, heaping teaspoons of sugar in his coffee, with Ted watching. Ted said, "Sewell, do you realize that you put three big spoons full of sugar in your coffee?" Sewell said, "Yes, but I didn't stir it!"

A short story I tell about myself (Ollie)

I had a hunter one time who used a lot of Creamora in his coffee. I decided to have some fun with him. One morning as I was preparing coffee, I exclaimed, "Someone left the lid off the Creamora jar, and now it's full of mouse turds." (I put a few speckles of instant coffee in the Creamora.) I carefully removed what the hunter thought was mouse turds. He drank his coffee black for the rest of the hunt. I never told him what I'd done. There is not a lot of profit margin in lion hunting, so I watch my expenses very closely!

Anonymous

I was camped in the White Mountains of Arizona huntin' lions. I told my helper to kill and butcher a deer for camp meat. I drove into town to pick up a hunter that was flying in from L.A. On the way to camp this hunter informed me he would eat everything but deer meat. He claimed deer meat wasn't fit to eat and would make him sick. I made no comment. When we got to camp, my helper had a delicious meal ready to eat (deer meat, of course). After dinner the hunter asked me what kind of meat we had for dinner. I told him it was goat meat. He said it was the best damned meat he had ever eaten. As soon as he got home he was going to buy some goat meat!

Some of Ollie's best dogs....

Abe

Maggie, Red and Blackie. These are crossbred hounds - the best bred to the best for over 100 years. Blackie is ½ Catahoula (a breed used in Spain for working cattle). He was a world class lion dog in every respect.

Hunter is "Arturo" from Sonora, Mexico.

Lion was caught in the Baboquivari Mountains.

Short Stories

Dad had a good hunting buddy by the name of Ed Donavan. Dad tells a story of when he and Ed went on a one-day rabbit hunt with their beagles in Northern Michigan. As was the norm, they left early and came back late.

As they were driving around looking for a place to hunt, Ed said, "Stop here, it looks like a good spot." Dad exclaimed, "Ed, it's posted 'NO HUNTING'." Ed went hunting anyway and dad stayed in the truck. After about an hour Ed returned with his scouting report. "Sign was right, Otto. There isn't any hunting there!"

I guess they had a rough trip and no luck. When they stopped at the café for supper (same one they had breakfast at) the waitress asked, "Any luck?" Ed immediately replied, "We had a good day. We got lost and we lost the dogs!"

****

Ollie Barney, my son, Allen, and myself were squirrel hunting on the farm one day. We have the California Rock Squirrel, and they are hell on pecans. Allen was real young and not doing any shooting, but he was counting. Ollie missed one squirrel with his .22-250 and then he got a chance to line up 2 squirrels and kill 2 with one shot.

When we got home Allen told his mom that Uncle Ollie shot 13 squirrels with 13 shots and only missed 1. Eileen looked puzzled for a minute, but it didn't take her long to figure it out. (Allen always called Ollie "Uncle Ollie" and his wife "Aunt Beryl".)

****

Ollie and I were raven hunting on the farm one day when I shot a raven with a shotgun and broke its wing. It was hopping around on the ground, and Ollie was glad to have the opportunity to shoot it on the ground with his .22-250. When he shot, he hit the second strand of a 4-wire barbed wire fence and broke it clean. "Not gonna make the rancher very happy, Ollie." Ollie finally got lined up with his moving target again and broke the fence a second time! "Ollie," I said, "If I were you I'd go buy a lottery ticket!"

****

    This story was told to me around a hunting campfire one evening. A hunter was deer hunting in Southern Arizona when he came across an adult female lion treed by five coyotes. He theorizes that the lion killed a deer and was feeding on the carcass when this family of coyotes showed up. When the coyotes started growling and yapping, the lion jumped up into a nearby tree. I never did find out the name of the hunter but I believe this story to be true. It is certainly believable by myself and others who know something about lions and coyotes. I am told the hunter had but one regret and that was not having a camera handy to take a photograph.

****

    Years ago I had a black Labrador retriever named Duke. His registered name was "Layne's Duke of Tucson".

    This dog was absolutely insane for hunting. I got him as a pup and spent a lot of time training him. He was so crazy for hunting that, if I were going deer hunting, or some other game that didn't require his help, I had to sneak the gun out of the house. He was a good house dog; the girls just loved him. He was also a good watchdog and a great hunting dog.

    When Duke and I would be on a water hole shooting doves, I wouldn't watch the sky. Instead, I would watch him. When he saw a bird (his eyes were much keener than mine), he would raise his head. I would get ready 'cause I knew a bird was coming. I tried to shoot them where they would land in the water 'cause he loved to swim.

    Duke always chased jackrabbits, but, of course, never caught one. I felt like it would be a dream come true if ole Duke could ever catch one. Out quail hunting one day we flushed a big old Antelope jack. I shot at it, but it kept running. I guess I must have wounded it or Duke would not have caught it. But he did, and what a sight! Seeing that dog carrying that rabbit! He jumped into the back of the jeep and stared at it all the way home! I always felt like I helped Duke's dream come true.

****

    Dove hunting one time I shot a weird looking dove. After close inspection I realized I had shot a cross between a Mourning dove and a White Wing dove. It was one solid color yet, much lighter than a Mourning dove. The feet and beak were shaped like a White Wing. I took it home and put it in my freezer to have it mounted, but I left it in there for too long, and it got freezer burned, so I had to throw it away. It was a beautiful bird and very unusual.

****

One of my favorite pastimes when my oldest daughter, Kelly, was 10 years old was watching her hunt on the Farm. I gave her a .410 x.22 magnum Savage over/under that she hunted with. I would drop her off in an open field with scattered brush piles from pecan trimmings. She would sneak around there and shoot quail, doves and rabbits.

She didn't like to waste ammunition. She would sneak up on them like she was stalking a trophy bull elk! She would line them up and shoot 2 or more at a time when able. I don't know of a better place to raise kids than on a farm with a gun in their hand.

****

A few years ago I bought a real accurate .223. It would shoot a 3/8" group at 100 yards easy. This was after I went round and round with the gun shop I bought it from. It wasn't right at first, but at my insistence they finally got it right. Dove season opened and I got a bright idea. I would shoot a limit of doves (10) with my new rifle and I'd shoot them in the head (sitting in pecan trees, of course). I shot the heads off 10 doves with 13 shots. This was the first time I was able to eat doves without worrying if I'd bite into a B.B. That was my last hunt with that .223. Some S.O.B. stole it from me. I hope I never find out who did. I enjoy my freedom.

****

Every 2 years I am required to get a physical to keep my pilot's license current. During my last physical, the Doc asked me if I ever smoked. I told him I quit cigarettes about 20 years ago, but I smoked an occasional cigar. He asked how many. I told him every time I caught a lion. He exclaimed, "I'll put you down as a non smoker!" Maybe he knows something about lion hunting!

****

Christmas morning when Allen was 8 years old, he and I made a token dove hunt on the farm before lunch. On the way home Allen was looking around for something to shoot at. We crossed a sand wash and Allen shouted, "Stop the truck, back up!"

"What did you see, son?"

"A bobcat!" He jumped out of the truck and bang!

I thought, "Oh great, Allen shot someone's house cat". But he didn't. It was a big tom bobcat with a perfect pelt. It looks like Allen might be as lucky as his Dad!

****

I owned a mule one time I called Helen Wait. I named her after a credit manager I knew by that name. Whenever anyone wanted to buy something from me on time, I would tell them to go to Hell and wait! This mule was such a good traveling mule that I changed her name to Helen Hurry. I sold her to Buck Garner. I should have kept her.

****

In April of 2002, I took Ken Ethridge, Jr., Carmen Miller, and Mark Helling on a one day lion hunt in Box Canyon. The dogs trailed a lion to the top of the mountain. When we caught up with the dogs, we all took a short break and dismounted our horses. Suddenly I heard a hell of a ruckus. I looked over at the horses and Cherokee, Ken's horse, was upside down with his feet sticking straight up in the air! He fell down and rolled completely over. I guess he fell asleep. I'm glad Ken wasn't on his back. Lucky Ken! (And probably "lucky" Layne!)

****

One day Mark Helling, Carmen Miller and I were returning from a lion hunt. Mark was closing a gate and Carmen and I were supervising the job. We were both sitting on our horses letting Mark do the work. Besides, the guide shouldn't have to do all the work! A car stopped (out of state tags) and a lady asked if she could take my picture. I was wearing my cowboy hat, chaps and spurs. (She probably had never seen anyone dressed like me.) I told her she could for $5.00. She stuck the camera out of the window, snapped a picture and sped off! One of the few times I've been robbed!

****

Everywhere I travel, I'm always looking at hounds. These dogs fascinate me. One day I stopped by a guy's house. I saw he had a lot of hounds, 10-15, I'd guess. I asked him what he was hunting with his hounds. "Oh," he said, "I hunt everything - lions, bear and coons." "How many lions have you caught with these dogs?" "None yet," he replied. (This ole boy could use some <u>good</u> <u>luck</u>.)

****

I have heard this story is true. I don't know the names, or where, or when. Take it for what it's worth...

This cowboy had an extra good looking wife. Seems when he was away, a peeping Tom would pay a visit. Taking matters into his own hands, he set a bear trap outside of his wife's bedroom window. When he caught the peeping Tom, he brought the culprit to see the judge.

The judge listened intently to both sides of the story. Then he made his ruling. "Ordinarily I would fine you for trespassing. However, I am dismissing this case."

He turned to the cowboy and said, "I know you are not happy with my ruling. The problem is, I have met your wife, and with the bait you are using, you might have even tempted the honorable court!"

I don't know what bear trap this cowboy used. If it was a grizzly bear trap like the one George Parker had, my guess is he was punished enough!

Allen Brandt (age 8) with Christmas bobcat.

Jeep Wreck

In 1976 Jim Smith and I decided to borrow my dad's Jeep and do some scouting for deer. There was an area in the Santa Rita Mountains that I wanted to look for deer. We left early Sunday morning and towed the Jeep to Patagonia. It was a nice September day, and Jim and I enjoyed the scenery. After driving up the mountain, we spent some time looking around. Life was good.

Around mid-day we started down the mountain. It was a very rough, steep road (or should I say Jeep trail?). Dad had just put new tires on the Jeep. This Jeep had oversized tires and undersized brakes...typical Jeep. This Jeep was a 1958 with no power steering and no power brakes, no roll bars, no top, and no seat belts. This old Jeep was a trick to drive, especially considering the fact that it would sometimes jump out of gear!

Coming down this mountain road, the right front tire caught the side of the mountain. The steering wheel spun to the right and almost broke my hand. I jumped on the brake pedal as hard as I could. The pedal was hard as a rock and the Jeep didn't even slow down. The Jeep was climbing up the bank with no way I could steer or brake. The outcome was obvious to me...the Jeep was going to roll over on its top. I hollered at Jim to jump out. Then I rolled out of the left side and scrambled back behind the Jeep before it rolled over on top of me. Jim was still sitting in the Jeep! "Get out of that Jeep before it kills you" I screamed! About that time Jim bailed out. I wasn't so afraid for my life because I felt sure I could get away from the Jeep, but I really thought Jim was going to meet his Maker. The Jeep rolled over on its top in the middle of the road. We walked out to the main road and were picked up by a couple in a pickup truck. They were good enough to give us a ride to Patagonia.

The next day we told Dick Walden (our boss) that we both needed a day off. (I'm not sure if we told him why!) As always, that was no problem. We took my 4-wheel drive Ford pickup with a winch and cables and jacks and come-alongs and you name it to help us turn the Jeep over on its wheels. It was one hell of a job. After I got home I telephoned dad to give him the news. He said, "Just fix it up in the same shape it was in when you borrowed it." Dad always was a bottom line kind of guy! I guess he figured if I could call him on the phone, I was O.K.

Jim left FICO in 1979 and we have kept in touch and remain friends til today. We are both lucky to be alive.

Smith Family 2000

Cowboy Humor

Manuel Sanchez has worked for my friend and ranching partner, Ken Ethridge, for approximately 30 years. Ken was killed in a truck accident in September of 2001. He will be missed by his family, myself, Manuel, and lots of other folks.

Manuel and a wetback were rounding up cattle one time and were camped out at a remote ranch. This wetback (Manuel referred to him as a "dumb wetback") kept pestering Manuel for a pinch of chewing tobacco. Manuel insisted he only chewed tobacco because it helped his English. Whenever Ken would come around, Manuel would put a pinch of chew in his mouth, making sure that the wetback saw him. (Manuel always talked to Ken in English.) After several days, the wetback told Manuel, "I would like to learn a little English myself. Would you sell me some chewing tobacco?" Manuel finally consented to selling a small amount for $5.00 (a tidy profit for Manuel). After a while the wetback asked Manuel, "Do I swallow this stuff or spit it out or what?" Manuel responded, "It's up to you. The more you swallow, the faster you will learn English." So the wetback swallowed it. By the end of the day the wetback was very ill and turning a light green color. He skipped dinner that night and went to bed. Manuel could hear him moaning all night. At 5:00 a.m. the next morning Manuel awoke the wetback to go to work. "It's time to get up and gather the cows. Answer me in English!" The wetback moaned, "Go to Hell!" and went back to bed. "See, "exclaimed Manuel, "that tobacco is working already!"

Manuel was gathering cattle along the River one day near Green Valley, AZ. An old man came by and asked Manuel if he knew what he was doing. Manuel replied, "The horse I'm riding is 25 years old and I'm 75 years old. Between the 2 of us we have been doing this for 100 years! You're damned right we know what we're doing!"

"On the wagon" in 1942 rounding up cattle in Sahuarita, Arizona.

Left to right: Sally Fletcher, Manuel Quiroz, Tom Wells, Angulo, Buck Fletcher, Chico Felix, Manuel Sanchez, Spicer and Mr. Ballard.

Manuel Sanchez was 15 years old in this photograph.

Manuel Sanchez 60 years later at age 75 still rounding up cattle in Sahuarita, Arizona.

One day Ken and Manuel were sorting cattle in a corral South of Tucson. There was a bull that kept getting in the way and causing a problem. Manuel roped the bull and threw the rope to Ken and told him to dally the rope and keep the bull away from the cows. Ken started to dally and tie this rope when the bull jumped over the corral fence. Somehow the rope got wrapped around Ken's waist and was pulled real tight. Ken hollered at Manuel to cut the rope. Manuel decided to untie the rope while Ken was gasping for air. After Manuel got the rope untied, Ken proceeded to eat Manuel's ass out. "I could have been killed" he exclaimed! "Well, Boss, I was just trying to save you some money. This is a new rope and you are always preaching at me to save money!"

In this case, Ken was lucky to be alive and Manuel was lucky to still be employed!

Ken Ethridge, Sr.

1921-2001

Del Goodin's Lion Stories

I first met Del about 5 years ago at a Pecan Growers' Meeting in Las Cruces, NM. He was about 60 years old at the time. It wasn't until April of 2002 that we had an opportunity to visit about lion hunting and ranching, etc. We had lunch at his home and his eyes lit up as he recalled some of his more memorable hunts. Del has hunted lions extensively in New Mexico and Arizona.

For 14 years he managed the Lynch Camp on the Diamond A Ranch in the Boot heel of New Mexico on the Mexican border. The Lynch Camp was about 51,000 acres in size. The Diamond A Ranch was about 320,000 acres. From his camp to the nearest town was 65 miles...long driveway.

I have always liked people who are kind to animals. Del has an old female Dachshund in his home. She is completely blind. He has spent over $1,000 on her medical bills and keeps her in the house because she knows where everything is. Only a true animal lover would have paid those medical bills. I know a lot of people that would have put her to sleep. Del is not a wealthy man, but he's made out of the right stuff.

One story that he told was when he was living at a ranch on the Salt River in Arizona. He was hired to do some predator control work for a ranch that was losing a lot of calves to lions. Three javelina hunters stopped by Del's house for a visit. They had seen his hounds and inquired if he hunted lions. After a short visit, he agreed to hunt with the 3 of them for 5 days. During that time he caught them each a lion and one of them a bear. He had a hard time catching the bear because his old trained dogs wouldn't take the track. He finally got a couple of young dogs to take the track. They caught the bear in a rock pile. It took until the following day to skin the bear out and pack out the hide. There was no way they could get the bear out in one piece.

While they were visiting about lion hunting, one of the guys asked Del, "If we start a lion track tomorrow, where will we catch it?" Of course, Del didn't have any idea. Del pointed to a small stringer of bluffs up the canyon. "Probably in those rocks," he exclaimed. The next morning the dogs hit a good track about 200 yards from camp. In less than an hour they caught the lion exactly where Del had said! Those guys were really impressed! (And, Del was really surprised!)

One morning in May, Del decided to make a token lion hunt. He invited his wife, June, along. June loved to go along and was a good hand. "I think I'll stay home. It's getting too hot. I don't think you'll catch one." When Del went to unleash his dogs, Tim, one of his best dogs, was sniffing the air like he was "winding" something off towards the mountain due west. Del rode in the direction Tim wanted to go. When they got to the base of the mountain, the dogs found where a lion had killed a calf. Tim had "winded" this kill from over a mile away! The dogs trailed up to the base of some big high bluffs. They tried and tried to find where the lion had gone. Del sat on his horse and watched for over 30 minutes. He was just about ready to call off the dogs, when one of the young dogs stuck his nose into a bush not more than 20 feet from Del. Out came this big tom lion! He had watched Del and those dogs for over 30 minutes! It didn't take the dogs long until he was caught. June was sure upset with herself for not going along.

Del saw his dogs trail a lion one time with 3 inches of new snow and no visible lion tracks. The dogs were smelling the track made before it snowed. (I have heard this from several lion hunters. I have never seen this myself.)

Del is lucky like myself and others. He has had a good dog, a good horse, and a good woman (not necessarily in that order). People like Del Goodin, Ollie Barney, Dale and Clell Lee, George Parker and others are the last of a dying breed. This world is a better place because of men like these, and I am fortunate to have known them.

Left to right: June Goodin, Dennis Rayburn, Dennis King and, guide, Del Goodin.

Big male lion caught by Del's best dog, Tim.

Record Book Cheetah

By Ollie Barney

In January of 2001 my daughter, Sherry Caldwell, and I traveled to Reno, Nevada to put together another hunt in the Dark Continent. We met with Roger Whittall who had five cheetah permits. I bought one on the spot.

I have hunted Africa six times and I have shot two leopards, two African lions, and I wanted a cheetah real bad. Every time before I hunted Africa, cheetahs were considered royal game, and we were not allowed to shoot one.

Sherry and I planned an around-the-world hunt in June. Our hunt started in Australia. We made two hunts there. Our first hunt was for four species of deer in the Southeastern part of Australia. We both shot all four species of deer each, and Sherry shot a water buffalo in addition to that.

After that we traveled to the Northern part of Australia, in the desert area, and hunted camels, wild donkeys and goats. There was a rancher there who had a permit to shoot kangaroos, so we got to shoot a couple of them.

After the Australian hunt, we flew to New Zealand where we hunted for tahr and chamois. We both shot good animals there.

Then it was on to Zimbabwe, South Africa. We were to hunt on the huge Humani Ranch. Sherry wanted to shoot a buffalo real bad. We rode around together for a few days, and I could see we weren't going to get a cheetah that way. Roger assigned me to an apprentice hunter. He said all we had to do was drive around in the grassland country and the cheetahs would hear us coming. They would sit up and look around, and we could get a shot that way. But, we were not having any luck hunting cheetahs this way.

This particular morning Sherry was not feeling well. She had a hard day the day before. My apprentice hunter and I were driving around and we found a huge wildebeest. My apprentice sure wanted me to shoot that thing. I didn't really want to, but I did. It was so big that the two black men, my guide and I couldn't load this wildebeest in the back of the truck. So we called Clyde (Sherry's guide) to come and help. On the way to us he drove past a water hole and saw two cheetahs getting a drink. He drove on by and called us, telling us where he was and for us to meet him. We drove back to meet him. I got in the back of his hunting truck and we went over to this tank - no cheetahs! Pretty soon two of them broke out of the brush and one of them started running straight down the road at a pretty good clip. They were around 50 or 60 yards before I got a shot. I hit him in the rear end, but I didn't break any bones. It went in his tail end and came out his side about where his liver is. Then as he was going in to some brush I got another shot at him, and hit him too far back. He went off just a short distance and went down growling and really complaining about it. My guide was about half-spooked of him, afraid he might charge us. He was real careful. The cheetah got up and I put another killing shot behind his shoulder. I don't know whether I'd have ever got a cheetah if I hadn't shot that wildebeest. We took it to camp, and Sherry and I took a lot of good pictures of it. We weren't allowed to bring any of it home 'cause they're illegal here in the States. As luck would have it, it was an extraordinary big cheetah.

Another group of hunters came in - there was 3 of them - and one fella was a taxidermist and an official measurer for Safari Club. He measured it up and according to his measurement, it would be # 2 in the Book. That pleased me real well because in '79 I was hunting there on this ranch during their civil war and I shot the #1 bush buck, but now he's down to about 4th or 5th. It only took me 29 years to get the cheetah I'd wanted.

Ollie Barney with daughter, Sherry Caldwell, and record book African Cheetah.
2001

Safari 2001 - Around the World in 55 Days
By Sherry Caldwell

Ollie and I had been talking about making another international hunt for years now. We had hunted South Africa in 1984, but for various reasons, we had been unable to schedule a trip until now.

I started to plan this trip in October 2000 by trying to contact the guide Ollie had used on two previous hunts in Australia. Peter Schultz was no longer in the business, so he referred us to an active guide he highly recommended, a man named Paul Convery. Paul sent us a video of his previous year's hunts and a lot of information about the hunts and facilities he could offer.

At first, we were primarily interested in the desert "varmint" hunts, but Paul had some interesting deer species available that neither Ollie nor I had ever hunted (or seen). We corresponded by email for several weeks and finally settled on a one-week deer hunt and a one-week desert hunt. We couldn't schedule the dates until we had attended the Safari Club International convention in Las Vegas in January 2001 and got a definite date for a hunt with Roger Whittall Safaris in Zimbabwe. While at the convention, we planned to check out the New Zealand outfitters. Since we would be in that part of the world and neither of us had ever been in New Zealand, why not?

As a reference point, I asked Paul if he knew any good guides in New Zealand and what the price ranges were for an interesting hunt. He responded that, other than himself, he couldn't think of a soul. It turned out that Paul had lived in New Zealand for 11 years and had been a meat hunter for five years. He also had done a fair bit of guiding during that time. The New Zealand outfitters at the SCI Convention were terribly expensive and we didn't like their policy of pricing the trophy fees based on where the animal scored in the record book. So we made arrangements with Paul to hunt Himalayan Tahr and Chamois with a colleague of his who provided helicopter hunts in the Southern Alps of the South Island.

We had scheduled June 3rd through June 18th for the Zimbabwe hunt so we back scheduled the Australian and New Zealand hunts to start in early May. As a little "vacation" to finish off the trip, we planned one week in and around London before returning home.

Roger Whittall insisted that a .375 was the minimum caliber he would allow for a Cape Buffalo hunt (using solids), so Ollie found me one and loaded up 70 rounds of ammunition for the hunts. He put my 4X scope on it and sighted it in for me. I target shot enough rounds to get over being afraid of it. It was too big for most of the game I would be hunting, but I didn't want to take two guns. I planned to use Ollie's 7mm Mag. whenever possible.

<u>May 3, 2001</u> (Day 1)

Today is my daughter Julie's birthday. That seems like an appropriate day to start an around-the-world trip. I checked my suitcase and backpack - I don't think I've forgotten anything important. I have one suitcase and the backpack. Ollie has one suitcase and the gun case. I think we are traveling pretty light for a long trip and three or four weather zones, but we have learned not to take more than we can manage by ourselves. Besides, on trips I never buy anything I have to dust or feed or might break on the way home.

Ollie's brother and sister-in-law, Dick and Betty Jo Barney, brought Ollie to Green Valley at 2:00 pm and Ollie, Damon (brother) and myself left for the Phoenix airport just before 3:00 pm. Damon dropped us off and headed home.

We started checking in with American Airlines for the flight to Los Angeles, with baggage checked all the way to Adelaide, Australia, when we hit our first snag. We were scheduled to fly on American to LA, then on Quantas for all flights through Johannesburg, South Africa. It turns out that Quantas has some severe restrictions on the transport of firearms and ammunition. Our counter agent called the AA Help Desk to get the proper procedures. The AA Help Desk called the Quantas Help Desk, who said the normal procedure was notification one or two days prior to departure for the transport of ammunition. And guns. We waited about 30 minutes while this conversation was going on. It was finally decided that the guns could go but not the ammunition. Our agent called and had our two suitcases returned to the counter since she had already sent them through the system.

We were very polite and very patient and refused to go away. I told her that waiting two or three days was unacceptable, and leaving the ammo wasn't an option. Guns and ammo just go together. Our agent, bless her persistent little heart, decided that she really needed to solve this problem. So she called the Quantas Manager of Dangerous Goods in Sydney, Australia. After she got him on the phone, she said, "Please talk to this passenger; she has lots of paperwork." I talked to Dan, who asked what we were about and where we were. I assured him that we had less than five kilos of ammunition in each suitcase. He pulled up our records, verified our itinerary, and said, "I don't see any problem; give me three minutes and I will add the authorization to your locator code. You won't have any question about firearms after this." It took about five minutes after that. Everybody was happy and our retrieved luggage was sent back again, along with the gun case.

In LA, when we checked in, they took our pocketknives and my cigarette lighter and sent them in a sealed packet labeled as "Security" items to be retrieved at the luggage counter at Sydney.

May 4 (Day 2-3)

We backed away from the gate at 12:01 am, Quantas 108 LA to Sydney. These are very comfortable accommodations. They served a meal they called "dinner" about 1:00 am our time. This is going to be confusing. Ollie passed on dinner but I had to at least give it a try. I was able to sleep or at least doze most of the time. Ollie did the same. We got breakfast about ten hours later. Wheels went down 14 hours and 12 minutes after rotation in LA. I don't feel jet lagged. We just chased the night across the Pacific. Dawn broke about two hours from Sydney.

Second snag - no suitcase in Sydney for Ollie. A suitcase that looked just like Ollie's kept moving around the baggage carrousel, so we figured out what had happened. My suitcase and the guns made it OK, so we filed a baggage claim and went on to Adelaide. I need to call Quantas as soon as we get to a hotel in Adelaide so they can deliver the suitcase.

As soon as we arrived in Adelaide, I called Paul to find what hotel was closest to him. He insisted that we stay with him. They have a one-bedroom unit, with bath, on the lower level of their home. Ollie's suitcase was delivered there about 5:00 pm.

May 6 (Day 4)

Since we crossed the International Dateline, we are now on May 6th. This is a "down day". We needed to loaf around and we did.

May 7 (Day 5)

Next snag - the local bank wouldn't cash our Traveler's Checks. They felt they needed "recourse" in case of a problem. I pointed out the 800 number that the bank could call to verify that the checks were genuine and not stolen, but to no avail. I think they just didn't want to do it. We ended up chasing all over Adelaide to find the American Express office that cashed checks. It took three hours but we were patient and successful. We've traveled before.

We had a good lunch and left for the hunting camp in Water Valley about 1:00 pm. We got there in time to take an hour or so to look around the area nearest the camp.

May 8 (Day 6)

We have seen more deer today than I have seen in all my years of hunting in Arizona and Mexico. Ollie agrees. I had one quick shot at a Red Stag that was running away from us, but missed. I could see by the look on Paul's face that he was thinking, "This is going to be a long hunt."

Tomorrow we're going back to see if we can find the one I missed. Paul also got the go-ahead to take a water buffalo, so that is on the list for me. It would be nice to get one when we can recruit some help from the station hands. Those buffalo are really big boys.

May 9 (Day 7)

After several hours of spotting and tracking Red Stag, we finally found one that Paul was happy with. It was another long shot and nearly dark, but that never bothered Ollie before. It didn't this time, either. He had a very awkward rest on the "bonnet" of the truck, but he still has the knack for getting a quick sight and shot. The stag is a very good representative of the species, certainly big enough to satisfy us, and we are all very happy with it.

May 10 (Day 8)

After a long chase and a stalk through the brush, I got a look at a good Fallow Buck. It was down the hill and then up a bit on the other side; about 200 yards away. I was lying slightly downhill and had to use Paul's jacket as a rest to get the gun barrel high enough. He whistled, the deer stopped and I shot it. We now both feel much better about my shooting skills.

Ollie got a really nice Chittal Stag. It wasn't too far from camp, either. It was a fairly long shot, but right on the button. As usual, any animal within 300 yards is in serious danger from my Daddy.

We decided that we also wanted to hunt Rusa Deer since there are a lot of good ones. They are native to Indonesia and have been imported to Australia for years. They seem to thrive and prosper in this climate. Ollie got his first. They are still in velvet but it is very hard and makes the antlers look unusual.

I finally got a shot at one but hit it a little low. It was a hard enough hit to put the buck down so I got up to it quickly to finish the job. It has very hard velvet on the antlers - makes them look white in the scope.

Again, we are happy campers. This is very different hunting for us since there are so many animals, really good bucks, that Paul has to choose what he thinks is the best. The others are "rats". We saw bucks that looked good to us and Paul would say "Nah, that's a real rat". So on we would go.

May 11 (Day 9)

We tracked for hours again today, mostly from the truck. We're looking for a Fallow Buck for Ollie and a Red Stag for me.

We finally started seeing lots of Fallow Deer and Ollie shot a good one. Paul wasn't as happy with it as he thought he would be, so when we found a better one he gave it to Ollie for his birthday. We had discovered that Ollie, Paul, Paul's wife Chris, and his son Gareth all have birthdays on either the 23rd or 24th of January. Mine is in May, the same month as Paul's daughter. She's in London, so I'm all alone with these Aquarians.

Anyway, the buck was moving at a slow trot about 300 yards away. Part of the deal was that Ollie had to kill it with one shot. He had a good rest on the bonnet and hit it through the heart. The deer still ran 125 yards after it was hit and then dropped. Paul accused Ollie of showing off. Ollie told him that if he (Paul) wanted this stuff to stay alive, don't tell him how to shoot! Paul can't wait to rag on younger hunters about this "Old Man of the Mountains".

Not long afterwards, we found a really good Red Stag with a dropped tine on the right. It was about the same size as the first one that I had missed, but had an interesting, atypical rack. The stag was about 200 yards uphill and facing me. I hit it right in the middle of the lower neck. It ran about 25 yards into heavy brush so we tracked it, and I was able to finish it with a second shot. Paul had pointed the stag out to me and then turned away and plugged his ears. He claimed he could feel the muzzle blast on his butt. I accused him of being too sensitive. We are VERY happy campers.

We went out again just before dark to look for a big Chittal buck for me (we had seen one the morning before in the area). We didn't get through the first gate away from camp before some bucks broke through the brush on the right. Paul told me to shoot the one on the left and I shot before he could plug his ears. That .375 with a muzzle break is a noisy puppy when it goes off close to your head. Paul's ears were ringing for hours. Maybe he's not so sensitive after all.

Paul was very unhappy with himself because the buck had a broken "inner" and was not a typical shape. He thought he should have noticed that. Everything happened so fast that I didn't know how he could have seen it. In any case, I like the size and shape of the antlers even if he doesn't. I killed it and it's mine.

<u>May 12</u> (Day 10)

Today is buffalo day. We found the big one we had been looking for all along. It was with two buddies. I shot him in just the right spot to bring him down and then was able to finish him with a second shot through the heart. We had to wait quite awhile before the other two moved far enough away that we could approach him.

It took several hours to process him because it was so big and Paul wanted the cape. We were careful with the meat and Paul pulled out the back straps for himself and family. Ollie and I would have loved to make jerky out of the rest of the meat, but no time for that. The station hands got a lot of stew meat instead.

We packed up that evening and headed back to Adelaide. Gareth had tied my buffalo horns to the front grill of the truck. Most of the rest of the deer antlers were tied up on top of the truck. We looked pretty wild coming out of the brush. Ollie is little deaf and Paul's truck is a diesel, so conversations were at a higher volume than usual. Paul would say something to Ollie in a normal tone and Ollie would ask him to repeat it. Finally Paul shouted: "The way we're yelling at each other, people are going to think we're married!" Ollie said that it was a good thing he couldn't hear everything Paul said because it would probably just piss him off.

It's hard to complain about 100% success for two hunters and five species, so we didn't. Ollie and I are having a great time.

<u>May 13</u> (Day 11)

Today is a quiet day. We all need some down time. Paul worked on the heads, getting them cleaned and boiled out. He'll ship them to us after we get home.

I caught up on the laundry. I also discovered that my ATM card works very well. I can trade plastic for Australian dollars with only a $2.00 ATM fee. That's a lot cheaper than paying a currency exchange rate. It kept telling me that I could have $1000 AUS but would only give me $950. I, of all people, should know that one can't trust a computer.

May 14 (Day 12)

Another quiet day. We had planned these in the schedule so Ollie and I could reset and Paul could work on the trophies.

May 15 (Day 13)

Today we drove north to the Timari Desert. It's in the northeast corner of South Australia, just south of the Simpson Desert in the Northern Territory. It's about a nine-hour drive. We saw a lot of country that looks like West Texas - miles and miles of ... miles and miles. When Ollie was here before, he hunted in the Simpson Desert.

We're staying at an old farmhouse and it's huge. It has six or seven bedrooms. The original walls are fieldstone and must be two or three feet thick. The temperature is so high here in the summer that they were needed just to survive. After sundown, it's like being in a cave. It's not all that bright during the day.

The station manager, Jason, is a young man who, with his wife Patsy and two year-old son Wally, has been here for about six months. Paul didn't think she was a very good cook, but Ollie and I didn't have anything to complain about. Chris and Gareth spoil Paul because they are very good cooks. Gareth did all the cooking during the deer hunt in Water Valley and we never had a bad meal. I have never drunk so much coffee or eaten so much bread in my life. I may have to go home as excess baggage.

The average rainfall here is two to four inches but it hasn't rained yet this year. The livestock all look fat and healthy and we can't understand why - we don't see anything edible. Paul says they eat dirt with sand for dessert.

May 16 (Day 14)

Today is camel day. Paul has been worried about this hunt because of the area we may have to cover to find them. Given our schedule (we have to be in Zimbabwe the 2nd of June). Paul could only allot three days to camels in order to leave time for wild donkeys and goats.

Jason went out early on his motorbike to see if some camels were still in the same general area where he had seen them earlier in the week. They were, so we headed out and found some in about one and a half hours. Ollie and I each got one but they are so massive I couldn't find the right spot right away. I had to shoot two or three times before I finally downed it with a shot through the shoulder and one through the neck. This camel is the largest animal I have seen, other than an elephant. Ollie's camel had broken its back teeth because there was no way it could close its front teeth together. Paul said that the bull camels are very bad-tempered and aggressive and that the injury was probably a result of fighting.

We wandered around a lot since it's interesting country; it's a very sandy desert with a lot of scrub brush. On the way back we came across a herd of 12 to 15 camels, then later saw a small group of four or five.

When we got back to the ranch house I showered and changed clothes. Clean clothes for my birthday tomorrow are a must.

We left a day early. We're off to find the wild donkeys south of here.

May 17 (Day 15)

Today I am 59. That's awfully close to 60. I guess I'll learn to live with it.

We headed south this morning to find the wild donkeys. Paul hasn't hunted this area before, so he is worried about the details of the lodging and hunting. He can't get the kind of answer he wants from the Station Manager - DIRECT! Paul says that this is a national trait of Australians that *drives* him crazy (more like a short putt in my opinion).

Ask a direct question: "How many?" Answer: "A few."

"Is that a couple?" "Could be."

"Is a couple two or three?" "About that."

"About two or about three?" "More than a fair number, but less than a mob."

The cottage we're staying in is somewhat of a relic, but it has indoor plumbing with a flush toilet. All houses have rainwater tanks to augment well water. The central section of Australia is a huge basin; only a few rivers and streams actually run into the oceans. There must be a large aquifer under the basin, but it also must be deep. The rainfall around here is not much higher on average than where we hunted camels.

The Station Manager is Gordon, who lives here with his wife, Lynn, and daughter, Ellen. Ellen takes school assignments over the short-wave radio and meets with her teacher from time to time. Next year she will be in the eighth grade and will start boarding school in Adelaide until she finishes high school. Gordon, his brother and his uncle tend a station of 1000 square miles. Many of the stations are that large, so local schools are not very practical.

Lynn and Ellen made a lovely dinner for us. Lynn had made a pineapple pie, so when she heard it was my birthday she put a candle on it for me. I had a birthday pie in the outback of Australia. That's a new experience.

Gordon's favorite joke: An outback farmer won the lottery; an enormous sum of money. When asked what he was going to do with all that money, he thought about it for a long while. Finally, he said, "I guess I'll just keep farming 'til it's all gone."

May 18 (Day 16)

Paul isn't happy with Gordon's hunting vehicle. He will get things changed before he comes back here. Paul, Gareth and I are in the back on a bench. Ollie is in the front seat. There is a metal rack around the truck bed that is exactly the wrong height for a rifle rest - too high if sitting down and too low standing up. However, we are nothing if not flexible.

Again, we saw very little that looked edible but all the livestock looked fat and healthy. Gordon told me that it had rained once and grass actually grew for one summer, so the critters were just living on memories.

We saw a big kangaroo and stopped to take a shot (Gordon had permits). Just as I was squeezing the trigger, Ollie shot. We both hit it - thump, thump. Paul said, "I can't believe that your own sweet daddy poached that 'roo right out from under you!" It turned out that Gordon, who was driving, told Ollie to shoot at the same time Paul told me too. Ollie always had a sensitive trigger finger.

We chased a large herd of donkeys for a long time and finally got within range. Ollie, Gareth and I each were able to kill two. I have great pictures of my "wild black ass". Gordon had a lot of wild horses - brumbies - that he would let us hunt but we declined. Two donkeys were plenty.

We decided to move on this evening. That gives us some extra time if we need it for the wild goat hunt. We headed south again to find a motel somewhere along the track. After stopping for diesel, the station owner told Paul a shorter way to get to Pitcairn, where we will hunt the goats. So, on we went. We arrived about 9:00 pm and set up camp in the old sheep shearer quarters. There are lots of small bedrooms with two twin beds in each one. There is a large, well-equipped kitchen and a refrigerator. There is also an old wood stove that was probably the original equipment for the kitchen. Also flush toilets (Ollie and I are getting picky in our dotage) just down the path from the rooms.

<u>May 19</u> (Day 17)

There are mobs of goats here. I shot one near the truck. Then Paul spotted a small mob of goats up on a hill about a half-mile away. We got closer and then went out to stalk them on foot. Ollie stayed in the truck since his knee was not going to allow that kind of hike. We climbed a steep hill and circled around behind them; it took nearly an hour and a half. I was winded - riding around in a truck for two weeks isn't very good training for this but I recovered and was able to make some good shots. Three goats with four shots. I was using Ollie's 7 mag since I was conserving ammo for my .375.

This is the prettiest country we have seen so far, although Water Valley is nearly the same. There are rolling hills, clumps of trees and scrub brush. The creek we go up and down has run once in the past ten years that Paul knows about. The station owner, Ross, said that they are in their sixth year of drought. He had to sell all his cattle three years ago. He now just runs sheep and the goats are serious competition for what little feed there is.

When we got back to camp for lunch (we rarely miss a meal) Ross' wife, Jean, had made a big pot of soup and a bacon and egg pie for us. Dinner included a fantastic cheesecake with double cream. This is turning out to be a REALLY good hunt. Ollie laughs at me. He thinks my mother should have named my siblings and me "Scout" since we always seem to be looking for our next meal.

We fired up the donkey engine to heat water for showers. I was first. The water kinda slushed out of the showerhead and was just warm enough to stand next to and slosh around. I managed to get fairly clean and wash my hair. I was chilly but felt a LOT better. I guess we didn't wait long enough for the water to get hot because Paul was next and I had used up all the warm water. He was cold! He would have quit but didn't want me to think he was a wussy. Gareth decided to wait and Ollie opted to skip it altogether. After a couple of hours of spotlighting for foxes that evening, Gareth had a nice hot shower. Patience is a virtue.

The shearer's quarters are not used much anymore but are very comfortable.

<u>May 20</u> (Day 18)

Today is goat day again. Gareth spotted some big billies we chased them until we got into range. Ollie did another one-shot kill. He's a tough act to follow.

The bigger one had taken off so we went in wild pursuit until I could get a shot. It was still moving pretty fast and I had to shoot twice before I brought him down. I decided to keep the horns, since they were fairly big and well matched. I had forgotten how bad billy goats stink.

We went back to camp to pack up and head back to Adelaide. Paul can't believe how we have been able to find everything we were hunting for and finish early. Ollie keeps telling him what a lucky hunter he (Ollie) is. Paul seems to have the same charm or animal magnetism or whatever it is that works. Some sort of pipeline to the Hunting Gods.

We weren't scheduled back until the 23rd so Ollie and I will have an extra day or two in Sydney. I can catch up on the laundry again and maybe find a dry cleaner. My sweater is in sad shape and our field jackets aren't any better.

We took Paul, Chris and friend/taxidermy helper Jackie out to dinner at a great steak house. It was quite a change from the bush/outback.

<u>May 21</u> (Day 19)

Ollie and I flew to Sydney and arrived with all luggage and guns. I found an apartment hotel with a washer, dryer and a kitchenette. I found a small market only five minutes walk away that also was a dry cleaner drop-off. I bought all I could carry back and we're all set for the next three or four days. We had a big lunch on the plane, so a light dinner and early lights-out was the plan.

<u>May 22</u> (Day 20)

Today is laundry day. The machines are about half size so this is going to take most of the day. At least it is more convenient than a laundromat, which I never found. Maybe I should have just had everything dry cleaned.

I need to find another ATM. Most places take MasterCard or VISA, but busses and taxis want cash.

Ollie's knee is very sore today. We'll get out tomorrow and do some sightseeing. I'd like to see the harbor area and the opera house.

<u>May 23</u> (Day 21)

We took a taxi to the harbor area - it's called the Circular Quay - and caught a tour bus. The Red Explorer. They run all day and make 25 stops around the city and a ticket lets us get on and off a bus at any stop. We got off at the Hard Rock Café stop so I could buy a shirt. Since the busses run every 18 minutes, we just walked back to the stop and caught the next one that came along.

It is an excellent way to see the city. The bus drivers are also the tour guides and know all about the places we go by.

We got off again at The Rocks, which is the first settled area; the first place the English landed in 1788. We went down to the waterfront and found a beachside restaurant. I had the lobster bisque and the bouillabaisse. Ollie had fried oysters. Mine must have been good because I got it on both of us. Everything was delicious, including the bread and beer. We like Foster's the best so far.

I skipped dinner and did some more laundry. I never did get all the soup stains out of my shirt. Oh well, it's old and I may leave it in Africa.

May 24 (Day 22)

I called brother Damon this morning. There are 17 hours difference and he's a day behind us. It's 9:00 am Thursday morning here and 4:00 pm Wednesday afternoon in Green Valley. He and Georgia haven't seen Cinco the cat for nearly a week and everybody is worried. All else seems to be OK.

Ollie and I took the Blue Explorer today and saw a different part of the city and harbor. It goes further north into the beach area. On the way out of the harbor we saw the USS Kitty Hawk and one of its destroyer escorts moored at the navy docks. They must have come in during the night. The Kitty Hawk had a deck full of Tomcat fighters. We saw US sailors all over the city and I think every bar or pub had a "Welcome US Navy" sign on it.

We had lunch at a sidewalk café across the street from the beach. Fish and chips and beer. Life is good! I bought a bunch of souvenir shirts for friends and grandkids so I had to buy a heavy-duty plastic bag for suitcase overflow. It's something I can check on the plane.

May 25 (Day 23)

I found a letterbox and mailed postcards. I also found a corner bistro that had an internet access machine (coin operated). I checked email and all is well.

We loafed around today and I did a last load of laundry. This is it until we get to Zimbabwe. Nothing is officially dirty until we get there; only previously worn. There is daily laundry service at the Whittall hunting camps.

May 26 (Day 24)

We flew to Christchurch today and met Paul at the airport. There was no problem with the guns this time. I had sent the firearms permits in late March with a check for the fee. When we arrived, the police officer remembered the name and check because they couldn't process it. He sent me to the exchange window for cash. Money may talk but cash screams!

Paul had brought another hunter with him for this adventure. He's a young Australian man whom Paul had guided before. Terry seemed a pleasant sort of guy, so we think this will work out just fine. We found a hotel with shuttle service and went on our way.

<u>May 27</u> (Day 25)

We took a four and a half hour train ride over some of the most spectacular scenery I have ever seen. We were on the Trans Alpine Railroad going from Christchurch to Greymouth over the Southern Alps. We were told that rain is measured in feet, not inches, in this part of New Zealand. There was lots of water in rivers, snow-covered mountaintops and long sandy beaches. In the lower elevations, it looked like rain forest.

From the train, we boarded a minibus for a three-hour ride south to Fox Glacier, on the western coast of the South Island. Paul couldn't remember the name of the hotel Chris had made reservations at, so the bus driver took us around to various ones until Paul found one he liked.

<u>May 28</u> (Day 26)

Ollie and I went together in the helicopter with Paul and pilot James. James can flat-ass fly a helicopter. He is also a hunter and the flying is so natural to him that he just hunts and the flying takes care of itself. We were close enough to the ground at times that I could see bird tracks in the snow. James has rotor clearance "feel" down to millimeters.

These are the most rugged mountains I have ever seen. Everything is straight up or straight down with lots of brush and powdery snow. There are some rock falls at least 2000 feet high or deep with huge icicles hanging off some of the ledges.

The hunting procedure is this: We fly around the 10,000 foot level of mountains that are just over 12,000 feet high and look for either Tahr or Chamois. When a good one is spotted, James will set down as close as he can on a ridge near the animal so the hunter can get out with Paul and try to get a shot. Sounds easy if you say it fast.

It turns out that James puts the right skid down on the edge of a ridge and Paul and I climb out on the skid and jump into butt-deep snow. The first leap from the chopper to the snow was an adrenaline RUSH I'll never forget. (Part of the thrill was knowing that there was nothing under the other skid but 2000 of air. The other part was wondering how in Holy Hell I was going to get back.) I climbed part-way back up the skid to pull the rifle out from under the seat, then we hunkered down while the chopper pulled up and tried to keep the snow and ice from the rotor wash from clogging up the scope or rifle barrel. Next I had to flounder through the soft snow and try to get some sort of rest so I could take a shot at the Tahr that was bounding down the mountain on the ridge across from us. I hit it twice and then it disappeared. James dropped back down immediately and picked us up in order to drop us off again on a ridge opposite from where we had last seen the bull.

I discovered how to get back in - I had to grab the skid and pull myself high enough out of the snow to get one foot on the skid, then reach up to open the door, push the rifle in under the seat, then climb the rest of the way back in and get the door closed. All while the chopper was wobbling just a little back and forth. I was determined to do this well. I was not going to give Paul a chance to talk about this chubby little old lady they had to leave on the mountain because she couldn't get back into the chopper.

Back to the hunt: Paul and I were just across a deep ravine from the Tahr, who had run into some brush. I finally saw enough of him to get a good neck shot and killed him. James whipped back down, picked up Paul and they headed off to find a Tahr for Ollie. While I waited for them to return, I moved around a little on the ridge. I moved slowly because it's hard to flounder around in the snow - one step is level and the next is hip-deep - and also because it's straight down on three sides and straight up on the fourth. Luckily for us, the weather was absolutely perfect. Cold at that altitude but no wind, snow, rain or fog. The sky was a deep blue. It was beautiful.

About 45 minutes later I saw the chopper coming back with a large bull Tahr hanging on a rope between the skids. Ollie had made a very difficult uphill shot - one, as usual - and had gotten a very nice trophy. James hovered over my Tahr and Paul got out to retrieve my trophy. Paul had to pull the animal to a fairly clear spot, tie the rope on it and wait for James to put the chopper down low enough for him to hook the rope on the carry-ring. Low enough meant almost on Paul's head. Then Paul climbed back in and they came to get me. I lost my hat from the rotor wash this time, but there's no going back since it went over the edge.

After James found a flat place lower down the mountain for a photo op we started out again looking for Chamois. When a group of good ones were spotted, James dropped the Tahr and started looking for a good place to drop us. This time Paul, Ollie and I all got out - a thrill a minute!! It was just as exciting the third time as the first! We couldn't see the Chamois after we were on the ground; they were across the ravine and straight up about 200 yards away in some heavy brush. We were looking into the sun, also. James immediately positioned the helicopter above and to the left of us so the chopper shadow would cover us. Finally one of the bucks stuck his head up a little and Ollie could see his head and part of his neck. Ollie made an absolutely incredible shot; he was lying on his back in the snow with the rifle nearly vertical and killed the Chamois with one shot through the neck. Paul was nearly speechless with amazement. Ollie is his HERO!

The second buck was in a brush cave and none of us could see him. So James picked Paul and me up and dropped us across the big ravine about 70 yards downhill and across a small ravine from where the Chamois was. I fired twice, but too low; all we could see was his breath when he moved a little. Finally, we could see part of his face and Paul said, "Screw it, shoot him in the nose." So I did. He tumbled down the slope nearly to the big ravine and not too far from Ollie's buck.

James came in to pick Paul and me up, then Ollie, then back for the Chamois. Paul had a tough time getting up to where they were because of the snow and ice on the steep slope. Then he had to wrestle them to a place where James could drop down low enough to pick them all up. We found a place for a photo op and went back after the Tahr. Paul is getting a lot of exercise today!

We were all JAZZED! Four good animals in two and a half hours. And I was still on an adrenaline high from the first jump! Ollie and I decided to have Paul do shoulder mounts on all four trophies.

<u>May 29</u> (Day 27)

This is a quiet day for Ollie and me. Paul went hunting with James and Terry, who was also successful on both Tahr and Chamois. Paul and Terry started skinning the six animals while Ollie and I supervised.

<u>May 30</u> (Day 28)

Ollie and I rested this morning while Paul and Terry went back to skinning. We were supposed to meet James at 1:00 pm but he called in early so we started out at noon. We still had one and a half hours of our agreed-upon six hours of chopper time. Paul wanted to get a Tahr and I needed another Chamois since my "nose shot" had gone down the side of the neck and ruined the cape.

I got out of the chopper with Paul when we spotted a good bull Tahr. Paul got him with Ollie's 7 mag, but took two shots. Ollie is worried about Paul's teaching the rifle bad habits. Paul and I and the Tahr were picked up in the usual manner. That's still pretty exciting, too.

We spotted some Chamois so Paul and I jumped out again. Same rush!! I'm getting hooked on adrenaline. The animals were hiding in the brush and we floundered around in armpit-deep snow until I could finally see a little patch of hide. I took one shot, then gave the rifle to Paul, who wanted to get a Chamois. He just kept looking into the brush and finally put the rifle down. He worked his way through the snow to the bushes and said, "You killed both of them with one shot! Is there no end to these Barneys?" He called me a greedy little girl! I told him I had to do something to keep up with my daddy.

Since we're leaving tomorrow we took the hides back to the motel and hung some of them up in the showers to let the water/fluids drain. I took a picture because it looked like we had killed and butchered someone in there.

May 31 (Day 29)

Today is a travel day back to Christchurch. First the minibus, then the train and back to the same hotel. We hung up the skins in the showers again - another photo op. This time we had small suites with kitchenettes so we boiled out the heads, too. We kept all the drapes closed so the maids couldn't see what we were doing.

June 1 (Day 30)

Our flight to Sydney is late morning, so I walked to the nearest store and bought 30 pounds of salt. Paul spread out a plastic tarp and re-salted the hides before we packed them back into heavy plastic bags (five of them). Paul borrowed a maid's vacuum cleaner so we could get rid of the mess (hide the evidence). He said that it's OK if they think we're trashy bastards, we just don't want them to know what we really are.

Since Ollie and I were flying business class we were able to check the five bags without paying excess baggage fees. Such a deal!!! However, when we got to Sydney we lacked another firearms permit to re-enter the country. After considerable discussion, the senior Customs Agent asked if it would be OK if they just stored the guns overnight for us since we were just in transit to Johannesburg. We readily agreed.

We said goodbye to Paul at the airport - he was on his way to Adelaide. We'll miss him. This has been one of the greatest hunts either Ollie or I have had. The weather has been perfect everywhere, the company was the best and the hunting was 100% successful.

I had picked a hotel out of the Sydney Yellow Pages for an overnight stay because it claimed to be close to the airport. It wasn't. Not only that, it was in a tough part of town and turned out to be a backpacker hostel! So much for random searches. The room was clean and comfortable, if somewhat small. Only one of us could stand up at once but we managed OK. I'm sure we woke everyone up when we dragged our baggage downstairs at 4:30 am to catch a taxi to the airport. C'est la vie!

June 2 (Day 31)

Another travel day. We claimed our guns from Customs and checked in for our flight to Johannesburg. We all wish Paul were going with us.

The plane was late in arriving; therefore it was late leaving. We have had so few delays in all the flights so far that we feel very fortunate. At this time we are 7 hours 25 minutes into a 14 hour 20 minute flight. HALLELUJAH!!! We're on the downhill run. This is our last Quantas flight; we're on British Airways through London, then American from London to Tucson. Ollie has figured out that we will have flown 30,000+ miles by the time we get to Jo'burg.

We checked into the Intercontinental Hotel across the street from the airport. It's brand new with good staff people and restaurants. It's close to five stars. This is the first hunting trip where I can take a hot bubble bath in a marble-floored bathroom. Life is really GOOD!

June 3 (Day 32)

We took our second malaria tablet today. I guess we need to do this. It seems to make me a little dizzy.

We fly to Harare today. We will be staying at Georgie Smith's B&B. I hope she meets us at the airport because I don't have her address.

Good News! Georgie and Anne Whittall both were at the airport to meet us. It was nice to see a familiar face. We paid out $30 US to get visas - gun permits were free. The economy seems to run on US currency. Even the government demands fees in dollars.

We had tea in Georgie's garden and met her mother. She is quite a character. We had dinner and went to bed early.

June 4 (Day 33)

Anne drove us to the Humani Ranch today. It takes four to five hours. The smog over Harare is the worst I have ever seen - even worse than what I saw in pictures of LA in the early fifties. Diesel fuel fumes, dust and wood smoke are the primary sources.

We arrived at the Turgue River camp at 1:30 pm. We met our hunter, Clive Halamore, whom we had met briefly in Las Vegas at the SCI Convention and his two trackers, Shortie and Piason. After lunch, we drove around and saw lots of game, but not what we are hunting.

June 5 (Day 34)

We crossed the Turgue at dawn to the Bedford hunting area to look for Cape Buffalo. We spent most of the day driving the perimeter roads looking for tracks. Humani Ranch is one of 19 farms that joined together to form a hunting conservancy of one million acres. Only the outer perimeter is fenced; all interior areas are unfenced.

We found some fresh tracks in the afternoon and followed them into the jungle. We found four bulls (they're called "duggerboys") but all were immature males. That means that the boss is soft in the middle and will boil away leaving a big gap between the horns. So we let them go. It would have been a clear shot with a good rest.

June 6 (Day 35)

We walked all morning, went back to cap for lunch and walked all afternoon. We didn't see any buffalo.

We had dinner with Roger and Anne Whittall at their house. It was a very pleasant evening. We met Daniel and his wife Dee there. Daniel is an apprentice Professional Hunter (PH). Dee works as general staff assisting all the hunting camps.

June 7 (Day 36)

We found buffalo during our morning hike; one big bull in a small herd. We had been walking for about four hours, then started stalking the group. We crawled through grass, brush and buffalo shit for several hundred yards. Clive was waiting for the bull to move from behind thick brush when four game scouts walked over the hill and spooked the herd. There must have been 70 or 80 animals in the group. They flattened the jungle; it looked like someone was building a runway. We followed for hours but never caught up with them.

Hilton and Raye came to the camp for dinner. He's a PH for Roger working out of another camp. It was a nice evening. We had Wildebeest Wellington. Yum!

June 8 (Day 37)

Today we found a large herd of buffalo. There were several hundred animals in groups of 30 to 50. We stalked one group for several hours but the biggest bull was immature. Paul would have called him a rat. We found another herd with a "shooter" but they spotted us and we had to freeze in place. Finally one of his wives or girlfriends warned the bull that he had better run, so they all took off.

Ollie went with Daniel today. He shot three impala for camp meat. He also shot a civet cat during the evening spotlight run.

June 9 (Day 38)

We stalked more buffalo on both morning and afternoon hunts. No shooters, though. Ollie went with Daniel again. He shot a monkey and a big dog baboon. I have seen mobs of Impala, Kudu, warthogs, baboons, some monkeys and lots of beautiful birds. No "shooter" buffalo.

We came across a King Cobra today. An eagle had broken its neck and then started eating it from the tail. It was about 1/3 eaten but was still alive. Clive told me there are six varieties of Cobra in Zim, two of them the spitting kind. If one spits, it aims for the eyes and is very accurate. The remedy is to wash out the venom with milk, water or urine (in order of preference). There is an acid in the venom that will cause blindness within 30 to 45 minutes. This might be more than I want to know. I also saw a Puff Adder.

<u>June 10</u> (Day 39)

Happy Birthday, Georgia!!

More hunting, no buffalo, no cheetah.

I saw Nyala today from the camp verandah. We can see the opposite side of the river from camp. Lots of game comes down to graze and water. There is a troop of baboons that lives on the riverbank below our hut and another troop just across the river. When the troops aren't quarreling among themselves, they shout insults at the other troop.

<u>June 11</u> (Day 40)

We were driving down the Bedford perimeter road at 6:00 am when Piason saw buffalo across the river. We took off boots and socks and rolled up pant legs and waded the Turgue. Shoes over the shoulder, rifle held overhead. The water was from ankle- to-thigh-deep and was 120 yards wide. The water was cool but not cold. We climbed up the bank, dropped shoes and started stalking the buffalo through the reeds and grass. Clive had set up the shooting sticks (a tripod of sorts) but the big bull stayed behind the thickest bush. He was with three other bulls and a lot of other cows and calves.

They scented us and took off. We thought they had left the area but when we moved forward about 50 yards they stampeded again. They thundered toward the jungle then suddenly turned towards the river. We ran barefoot through the underbrush to the river's edge and watched them going across the water about 300 yards downstream from us. They came up against a bluff and couldn't climb out so they turned left and ran up the river toward us. When they were exactly opposite us, 120 yards away, we were looking directly into the sun and couldn't see them anymore.

The lead cow stepped into a hole and went into water nearly over her head. She knew the calves couldn't make it so she turned to come back across the river. Four young bulls managed to climb out a less-steep bank and stay on the other side. The big bull and his three buddies stayed with the herd. When he was as close as I thought he would get, I took a shot. He was lunging through the water and I hit him too high on his back. He bled enough to leave a light blood trail.

We put on our boots and stalked the four bulls for the next ten hours through grass and brush higher than our heads. It was spooky. I walked about five yards behind Clive so we would both have a field of fire if the bull ever turned and charged us. After four hours, we caught up with the four bulls, which had split away from the herd, but the jungle was too thick to identify which one was mine. It was also impossible to get a clear shot. They ran and we followed again. We found them once more, but the same thing happened. By now, I was hoping they would charge; at least I could get another shot. I think. The jungle was so dense in places that they could have been six feet away and we wouldn't have seen them.

At near dark, we waded the river again and went back to camp. I was so disappointed in myself for making such a poor shot. I was also tired. A Diet Coke and a little water don't last all day.

June 12 (Day 41)

We went back to the same place we first saw the buffalo along the river and waded across. We zigzagged across the area where we last saw the four bulls, but no sign. They must have doubled back and crossed the river.

After lunch we started searching for tracks on the Bedford side of the river. We found some and followed for several hours. We were downwind and nearly walked into them before realizing they were there. We could hear them moving a little, we could even smell them, but couldn't see them. They were maybe ten or twelve feet away and didn't know we were there. Clive motioned for me to get my rifle ready to fire because if the nearest bull moved out onto the path we were on, we would have to flatten him. We had nowhere to go. Shortie and Piason, in front of us, started to kneel down so we could shoot over their heads. Shortie was just about to squat on his heels when we heard a SSSSSSSSSST. We all went ooooooooh and the buffalo stampeded off to our right. It was a large Puff Adder. We abandoned ship.

We followed the bulls for a while but it was getting late and we had a long way to go to get back to the truck. Shortie found some blood on a stalk where the bulls had been lying. On the way back to camp we saw five elephants, two cows with calves and one young bull.

Ollie went spotlighting. I went to bed.

June 13 (Day 42)

I had an upset stomach this morning, so Clive, Shortie and Piason went to see where the four bulls had gone. They found that the buffalo had crossed the river again to return to their normal feeding grounds close to the jungle. Ollie went out with Daniel and shot a huge Wildebeest.

They called Clive for help and on his way to them he saw two Cheetahs at a waterhole. He radioed Daniel to bring Ollie quick! They met and Ollie got into the back of Clive's truck and headed for the waterhole. It looked like both cats had left but suddenly one of them walked out and started running down the road ahead of the truck. Ollie had to do a "Texas Heart Shot" and missed a perfect shot by half an inch. The Cheetah slowed down but kept moving. He had one more quick shot through the body that sent it down. He finished it with a third shot.

They came back to camp all JAZZED!!! It was a big cat and they couldn't wait to measure it. It is seven feet one inch tip to tail and weighs between 115 and 120 pounds. It will easily make the book and so will the Wildebeest. This is a real trophy day for Ollie. This makes the hunt for me.

Four new hunters and two more guides joined us in camp. We had roast Warthog for dinner. Too much good stuff!

June 14 (Day 43)

We prowled around all morning, but no buffalo. We stalked a small group of Water Buck but didn't see anything worth shooting.

In the afternoon we drove the perimeter roads again. We started on the Turgue Camp side and were stalking a small herd of buffalo when we came across an elephant. It didn't scent us and kept on feeding. It broke off a tree branch bigger around than my thigh that spooked the buffalo into a full run, but only for a short distance. We followed and when we got close Clive climbed a tree to find out where they had gone. When he got up high enough to see, he found that a young bull was looking straight up at him. The grass was so tall that all Clive could see was his face and horns. They really spooked then but my bull and his three buddies split away from the rest. We tracked them for several hours but the jungle was just too thick. Then we ran on to the elephant again and had to abandon ship.

We had Impala roast for dinner, compliments of Mr. Barney.

June 15 (Day 44)

We hunted hard all morning but again no luck. At near dark we went back to the river to try to catch the buffalo going to or from the water. Again, no luck. They didn't show before it was too dark to see.

We had Impala stew for dinner. Everything is good.

June 16 (Day 45)

We were at the river at first light but no buffalo were there. We hunted for several hours and ran across a really nice bushbuck. So I killed him. My first African trophy on this trip.

We saw a herd of buffalo on the way back to camp. We got out and stalked them for a fairly short distance and tried to get set up for a shot. They were moving too quickly by then, so I didn't even try. This has not been my lucky hunt. I'm really glad Ollie has gotten two record trophies.

June 17 (Day 46)

Clive left today for a hunt in the Upper Zambezi Valley. Roger had told us that this would happen when we booked the hunt. Ollie and I went out with Shortie and Leymon, another apprentice PH, looking for bush pig. We found tracks and sign but no pigs.

June 18 (Day 47)

We made another quick bush pig hunt in the lagoon area. We saw no pigs but Ollie did shoot another big dog baboon. We left for Harare after an early lunch. Charlene, the wife of PH Peter who was with Clive, drove us there. We went back to Georgie's B&B and it felt like home.

June 19 (Day 48)

Georgie took me shopping. I had to buy a big sports bag to replace the plastic one I had bought in Sydney. It held the entire suitcase overflow after I bought more souvenir shirts. It cost $700 Zim bucks. That is roughly $6.00 US. It's important to convert quickly before sticker shock takes over.

Charlene came back to take us to the airport. She has the ranch minibus and it's a lot easier to haul the gun case around in it. We paid our $40 US Departure Tax and caught a one-hour earlier-than-scheduled flight to Johannesburg. Our flight to London leaves tonight about 8:00 pm and we can wait in the BA Lounge. This is a First Class leg so the service will be good.

June 20 (Day 49)

We landed a few minutes early. The seats reclined to an almost flat position, so I was able to rest. The recliners were a little short for Ollie but he made the best of it.

The suitcases and gun case had been marked with firearms tags for special handling. When we went for the baggage, we found the sports bag only. I went to BA Customer Service and there were two BA Special Baggage handlers with Ollie's suitcase and the gun case. My suitcase went somewhere else in the world. BA folk escorted us to British Customs where we learned that my information was wrong - Customs will NOT store firearms for short periods. After 45 minutes of "sorting" things out, Customs gave us two options: get an airline to store them or get a local, licensed firearms dealer to come get them, store them for a week, and then return them to us. Soooo, back I went to BA Customer Service and recounted my sad tale of woe. The BA agent called BA Security and they said .....No Problem! They came to Customs, picked up the guns and told us to have American Airlines notify them when we checked in for our flight to Chicago. I LOVE British Airways!! We could have had anything in the suitcases. Not one customs agent even looked at my backpack once we said that we had firearms. I filed a missing baggage claim and we headed for the train station.

The train to Paddington Station was fast; then we took a taxi to the hotel. It was the opening day of Parliament so traffic was worse than usual. The streets around Buckingham Palace were closed.

When we got to the hotel, a Comfort Inn, Damon was there to meet us. The rooms seem small but all three of us can stand up at the same time in the same room. Better than the backpacker's hostel in Sydney.

June 21 (Day 50)

We took the Big Bus tours of London - all three of them. That is a really neat way to see the whole city. It took all day and we saw all the major attractions. We didn't walk much because both Ollie and Damon have bum knees. The weather couldn't be better. It is sunny and warm with a cool breeze. Damon never experienced this kind of weather in all his trips to London before, even when he stayed once for two months.

June 22(Day 51)

Today is Channel Day. We took a taxi to Waterloo Station and got on the Eurostar. Due to heavy train traffic, there were several delays along the way to the English Channel so the trip took a little longer than planned. It didn't matter to us. The "under Channel" time was 23 minutes and we estimated that we were going about 100 mph.

We got off in Calais, France and found that the station is out in the middle of nowhere. The dispatcher was kind enough to call a taxi for us and we went to a large mall where we had lunch. With lunch we had a French beer - it was no better than the New Zealand beer - basically swill.

The "under Channel" time on the return trip was 21 minutes. The really fast times on the train are between Calais and Paris but we didn't want to take the time to go that far.

June 23 (Day 52)

This morning we took a taxi to King's Cross Station and caught the train to Edinburgh. I'm sure the driver cheated me on the change. I guess it's not a real trip until a cabbie shortchanges one.

The countryside is many different shades of green and brown with low, rolling hills. We passed five nuclear generating plants, one with 12 cooling towers. The train was going as fast as the Eurostar; it's 395 miles with six stops in just less than five hours.

We arrived at the Waverly Station in Edinburgh and surprise! No taxis! There was a parade or march nearby and the cabs couldn't get down to the station. We walked to a nearby corner and finally found one.

We found a tour bus and rode it twice. The old city has some truly interesting features and monuments. It is much more gothic with spires and fretwork than London. We stayed at the Cairns (pronounced Kerns) Hotel. We walked around the corner and did a little Pub Crawling. We learned in London that Pub food is probably the best available and the same is true here. Fish and chips and beer! At 11:00 pm it was still light enough outside that I could read my watch without turning on a lamp.

June 24 (Day 53)

Ollie and Damon weren't up to a walking tour so we ate breakfast at the hotel and went to the train station. We caught the

9:30 am train and arrived at 1:15 pm. That meant speeds were at least 100 mph along the way.

The weather continues to be perfect. In London, we went to "our" pub for a late lunch but there is no food service on Sunday. So we toughed it out with a couple of brews - Foster's on tap, of course. A nearby restaurant was open for dinner.

June 25 (Day 54)

This is what cruise directors call a "leisure day". I need to sort out and repack all my stuff. I have lots of treasures now, mostly souvenir shirts. Remember the "No dust, No feed" policy! I would like to get the suitcase a little lighter, but I think it's hopeless.

We met Paul Convery's daughter, Reanna, for dinner. She's a sweetheart, which we suspected she would be. Ollie didn't like dinner, also no surprise.

June 26 (Day 55)

When we checked in with American Airlines, they told us that British Airways had delivered the gun case already properly tagged for Tucson via Chicago. Love BA!

We left just a little late but landed in Chicago on time. US Customs cared not a whit about the guns but were very excited about our having been in a Foot-and-Mouth contamination zone (Zimbabwe). They routed us through the US Agriculture Station so our shoes could be scrubbed. Again, no one even looked at our suitcases. They didn't even check the serial numbers on the rifles! We must not look like smugglers.

The flight to Tucson was on time and Dick and Betty Jo Barney met us at the airport. This was a hard day for Ollie because of all the walking we had to do. We were both very tired since traveling West makes for a really long day.

June 27 (Home Again)

So the journey ends. We flew over 40,000 miles and traveled thousands more in buses, trains, and hunting vehicles. We saw some of the most beautiful landscapes in the world and met people that we want to see again and again. Ollie collected some world-class trophies and fulfilled a decades-long dream of hunting Cheetah. I can't remember all of the people who told me that they wished so much to have been able to make this kind of trip with their fathers. I think I'm the luckiest woman on earth to have had this opportunity. If I hadn't taken a single trophy, it would have been worth everything it cost in both time and money. I wish all readers of this journal the same opportunity with someone they love.

Sherry Caldwell with Australian Fallow deer.

Sherry with Australian Axis deer.
2001

Guide with Sherry Caldwell and Himalayan Tahr.

Sherry with New Zealand Chamois

Mexico Dove Hunt

One Saturday in September, many years ago, Dad and I decided to spend the day dove and quail hunting along the Mexican border. I used to hunt birds a lot before I started lion hunting. We had my Labrador named "Duke", and we were going from stock tank to stock tank shooting birds and looking over new country. We were not paying very close attention to exactly where we were, but we knew that we were close to Mexico. We were a long ways from civilization and just having a good time. We had shot a lot of birds. I don't remember what the limit was back then, but you could shoot a lot more than you can now. We were shooting Mourning Doves, Whitewing Doves, and Gamble's Quail.

When the sun had set, we decided to head for the barn. We didn't go back the way we went in. We took the first road heading in the direction we needed to go. After several miles, I realized that we were in Mexico, southwest of Sasabe! We had two choices; one was to drive for hours and back track, and the other choice was to go through the checkpoint at the border. We decided to hide the shotguns and birds (as best we could) and go for the border. When we got there, the Federales tried to flag us down. I just kept driving and pretended not to have noticed. We were lucky that they didn't start to shoot at us. When we got to the U.S. side we told the U.S. Customs what had happened. He said, "I don't want to hear it. Just get the hell out of here muy pronto!" That was a real lucky break for us. Anyone who has known me long knows that I am a very lucky person.

Nevada Lion Hunt

By Ed Tomary

A gentleman by the name of Horton Bungardner owned a ranch in central Nevada called the Hunt's Canyon Ranch. This ranch had a history of lion problems. I told Horton that if he ever found a fresh lion track or a fresh kill that I would help him catch the lion. One winter day in 1972, Horton called me on his mobile phone. He said that he had just seen a lion cross the road in the vicinity of Salsbury Canyon. I told him to wait there for 45 minutes and that I would be there with some hounds to try to catch the lion. Horton said he couldn't wait. He needed to make his rounds to break the ice so that the cattle could water. I called around to find a hunter, but was unable to find someone on such a short notice. I decided to take four dogs (I owned 16 at the time), and my wife and I drove to the spot that Horton had described.

When I got there I looked around for tracks. What I found was hard to believe. There were five different sets of lion tracks between five and ten yards apart. All the tracks looked like they belonged to adult lions, and they were all going the same direction. One track was larger than the others. It looked like a family of lions. These tracks were heading into the lower country. I drove down to the next road below to check for tracks. The lions did not cross that road, so I drove back to where I saw the tracks. I told my wife to wait in the truck, and I would have a look around. I walked about 150 yards up the hill and then, all of a sudden, one of the lions jumped out of some bluffs over my head and ran down the hill! I fired two shots from my pistol, but I didn't hit the lion. The lion ran right past the pick up. My wife turned the dogs loose and the race was on. In a short while I could hear the dogs barking treed.

When I got there I saw that the four dogs had all five lions in the same tree! I took a picture of the five lions. I decided to shoot the female lion, which was stone gray colored with white markings. She was a beautiful seven-foot long female lion. She was the best looking lion of the five. I believe the lions were an adult male, an adult female, and three grown kittens. After looking around, I found where these lions had killed a mustang.

Several days later, one of the neighboring ranchers by the name of Albert Hooper congratulated me for killing this lion. Word travels fast when someone kills a lion. He commented that he was sure glad that lion wasn't going to kill any more deer. I did not tell him about the lions killing the mustang. However; a short time later, Albert found out from someone else about these lions killing the mustang. The next time Albert saw me he chewed my ass out for killing the lion. He did not like mustangs and he did not approve of someone killing a lion that was killing mustangs! Seems like it's damned if you do and damned if you don't in this lion hunting business!

Authors note: Ollie and I caught two lions in one tree once. Clay Howell caught a lion and a bobcat in the same tree off a kill one time. This is the only time I ever heard of anyone catching five lions in one tree. Ed Tomary was going to try to find a photograph he took of these 5 lions. I haven't received it yet. However, I have talked to people who have seen the photograph. I am 100% confident this is a true story.

Mexico Turkeys I

Many years ago, Dad and I and a mutual friend, Jim Russell, traveled to Chihuahua, Mexico to hunt the big Gould turkeys in the Sierra Madre Mountains. It was in the spring of the year and the turkeys were gobbling.

We met our friends Jay and Lorrell Clark in Colonial Juarez, Chihuahua, a small farming community at the base of the mountains. We enjoyed some good, real Mexican food and friendly small town hospitality. Lorrell and Jay worked for F.I.C.O. at one time and they were old friends of mine. We reminisced about old times and planned the turkey hunt.

The first morning we traveled to the top of the mountain to a place called "El Gavilan". We made camp near an old abandoned airstrip near some big beautiful tall ponderosa pine trees. That evening we drove around on some old ranch roads and listened for turkeys gobbling as they ascended to their roost trees. Just before dark we heard a turkey gobble.

Daylight found us near the roost tree. Jay was the caller and I was the designated shooter. The big turkey gobbled when he left the roost. Jay chirped on the call and the gobbler came on the run. At about 20 yards he stopped and started to strut and looked around for the lovesick hen. What he found instead was some BB's from my full choke 12-gauge shotgun.

At that time, I kept a shotgun in Mexico. I also smuggled in another shotgun tied to the frame on the underside of my pickup. I wouldn't recommend trying that today!

After we field dressed my gobbler, we returned to camp where master chef, Jim Russell, prepared a delicious breakfast complete with bacon, eggs and Mexican style coffee. Jim is an excellent camp cook. Our camp compared to a five-star restaurant in the meal department. Jim even made roast turkey for dinner complete with stuffing and cranberries.

We were having a great time: getting up early, going hunting, returning to camp for breakfast or lunch, taking a siesta, then hunting or fishing in the afternoon. (There were some small native trout near where we camped.) Life was good.

After a few days, Jay announced he was out of Coca Cola. He was going home. He told us we could stay as long as we wanted to. The ranchers on all sides of us gave Jay permission for us to hunt. I don't remember how many turkeys we had already. We had all shot at least one good turkey several trout. We decided to hunt for a few more days another turkey or two.

Jay left and we retired to our camper for our mid-day siesta. We had no sooner fallen asleep when we heard someone outside. I peeked out and saw an official of some kind riding a Mexican mule. Dad and Jim decided I spoke the best Spanish of the three. My Spanish isn't very good. I stepped out and introduced myself. The official asked to see our "permisimo de cocino and permisimo de rifle". I told him we didn't have any turkey or gun permits. He kept asking the same thing over and over. Finally, I returned to the camper to explain the situation to Dad and Jim. Dad said, "Tell him we are fishing!" I told Dad that would be a hard sell with the turkey capes and shotguns in camp! After much discussion, and reviewing our options, we decided to break camp and leave. We would always have one man near a shotgun at all times. We were quite sure that one Mexican with a pistol would not try to overpower three gringos with shotguns. We loaded up everything, then picked up the shotguns and loaded them in the cab. He never made a move. We were sure glad. We were not looking forward to a shoot out.

We quit the mountain and headed for the border. We were concerned someone may have radioed ahead to notify someone at the border. We crossed into New Mexico without a problem. The United States sure felt good!

We learned later that the reason the Federale was questioning us was because they were expecting a drug deal to occur on the runway and they wanted us to move. They didn't care if we hunted turkeys. I really need to work on my Spanish!

I enjoy Mexico and the Mexican people. It is a fascinating land.

Note: Mexican style coffee is when you put the coffee (preferably Combate) in a sock. Then you hold the sock over your coffee cup and pour hot water in the top of the sock. This coffee can be so strong that it takes a <u>lot</u> of cream to color it white.

Master Chef Jim Russell

Author with Mexican Gould

Mexico Turkeys II

Dad and I made another trip to Mexico some years later. I wanted to take Dad down there one more time before he got too old.

When we were at the border getting our Visa's and car papers, the Mexican official asked Dad if he had a notarized letter of permission from his wife to drive her Blazer into Mexico. Dad was dumbfounded! Seems the title to the blazer was in Mom's name. Mom and Dad never worried about whose names were on what. They figured they were legally married and everything belonged to them jointly. I didn't want to turn around and go home; I wanted to shoot a turkey. I took the title and went outside. I told Dad, "You wait here." I took a $20 bill and went back inside. I laid the money and the title on the official's desk. A car permit was granted! The Mexico bribery system was working perfectly!

We had a great hunt and called in a lot of birds. However, our shooting wasn't very good and a lot of them ran off. (Unless a turkey is shot in the head, they are extremely hard to kill, especially the big Gould turkeys.)

When we got back to base camp in Colonial Juarez, Lorrell Clark told everyone that you can't kill turkeys this time of year!

One of the reasons I quit hunting in Mexico is because of the heavy drug traffic. I was told that one of the ranchers down there owned a ranch in the path of a smuggler's trail. One day one of the main drug dealers paid a visit to the ranch owner. "This is a very nice ranch," he exclaimed. "We would like to buy this ranch. We can either buy it from you or your widow."

I have always enjoyed Mexico: good people, good land, good water, lousy government.

Mexican Lion Hunt

Ollie always wanted to visit Colonial Juarez, Chihuahua, Mexico. I had friends living there, so we decided to take a little vacation and drive down there and have a look around. We knew it was illegal to shoot lions in Mexico, so we took a few dogs with the idea if we caught one, we'd let it go. When we crossed the Border into Mexico at Agua Prieta, the Federales wanted to know why we were taking dogs. We had our rabies certificates, so we were O.K. there. We told them we were going hunting for "mapachas" (raccoons in Spanish). They didn't even know what they were. They said they wanted to see our gear and have a look at the dogs. When those hounds saw those Mexicans opening the camper door, they threw a fit. On the strength of that, they decided everything was fine, and they didn't need to look in the camper after all!

We had a pleasant drive to Colonial Juarez where we met my friend, Max Spilsbury. We spent the night and had a nice visit with his family. The next morning we got supplies and headed for the hills. We stayed at a ranch owned by the Whetten family, called the Stairs Ranch. Jay Whetten met us there and we made camp. It was a big house and very comfortable - a great camp!

This ranch used mules to work cattle instead of horses. It is rough country. The mule I rode they called "Ormega" (ant in Spanish). She was a little mule and my feet almost touched the ground. I was afraid I might get a snake bite riding her! But she was one tough little mule and had a big heart.

The first morning I saddled up and was ready to go. The cowboy (I can't recall his name) came by to check my saddle. He asked if my cinch was tight. I assured him it was. He took one look at my rear cinch and gave it a jerk. He tightened that cinch so tight I didn't think Ormega could breathe. They don't use britchens or croupers down there. They just tighten the cinch. Saves money, I guess.

They had a little hound down there they called "Jesse". He looked like a cross between a Black and Tan and a Beagle. He was the toughest little hound I ever saw. He didn't pack one ounce of fat. Every track he found, he would trail it for about a ¼ of a mile. If it went up a tree, he barked at it. If it didn't tree, he looked for another track. He would trail anything - deer, lion, bear, you name it. He was a lot of fun. They have caught lions and bear with Jesse all by himself.

The third day of hunting, the dogs trailed up a lion and jumped it in some rocks. They had it treed in no time. When Ollie and I got there, the cowboy and Max and Jay were already at the tree. The cowboy said, "Dos leones en la piña, muy alto!" (Two lions in the pine tree up high.) We looked and looked, but we could only see one. We thought maybe that cowboy was seeing things. After awhile we could just see the tip of the tail of the second lion. If it wasn't for that cowboy, Ollie and I would have caught a lion and wouldn't even have known the other was there!

We had a good hunt and a good visit. We got to tour a brand new horseshoe manufacturing plant. Ollie got to visit with the family of a man that was a friend of his and was killed in WWII. We got to listen to Dave Spilsbury, Sr. tell hunting stories.

On the way home, we saw what looked like junk cars on the side of a mountain. When we got to the area where we thought we saw the cars, we stopped to look around. There was a very sharp hairpin curve in the road. The road came right to the edge of a steep hillside. There were over a dozen cars piled up there over a period of time. There was a sign that said "dangerous curve", but no guardrail or anything. No telling how many people were killed there.

Several times on the way home Ollie would say, "I wonder how many lions I have gone off and left in those big tall pine trees over the years!"

It was a great time for Ollie and I. Good friends, good hounds, and good mules. We enjoyed our trip to "the land of mañana". The Sierra Madre Mountains are a very interesting piece of real estate. It was easy to see why it was one of the last areas in North America where grizzly bears became extinct.

Ollie and Layne's lion dogs in Mexico.

Lucky Pilot

I don't remember what year George Parker told me this story, but it's worth repeating.

George wanted to go to Mexico and shoot some turkeys. He hired a pilot (whose name I can't recall) to rent a Cessna 182 and fly him down there. They landed in Casas Grandes, Chihuahua, and George had a friend pick him up there and drive him to the mountains. George told the pilot to fly to Chihuahua City and fuel the airplane. He told him what day and time to be back at Casas Grandes to pick him up.

At the appointed hour, George met the pilot and off they went. After they had been flying for awhile, George noticed that the fuel gauges registered less than ½ tank of fuel. George quizzed the pilot. The pilot told George he did not go to Chihuahua City like he was instructed. "No need to. We have plenty of fuel to make it to Douglas, AZ. We need to clear Customs there, and we'll fuel at that time." George was not very happy. The headwind was much stronger than anticipated. About 50 miles before Douglas, they ran out of fuel. They made an emergency landing on a ranch road. A rancher came by in a couple of hours and gave them enough auto fuel to get them to Douglas (182's will run on car gas reasonably well.) They cleared Customs and bought fuel and went home.

When George said farewell to his pilot, he said, "That pilot's license of yours doubles as a good luck charm." "Why is that?" inquired the pilot. "Because," explained George, "If I knew how to fly, the buzzards in Mexico would be feeding on your carcass right about now!"

For those of us who knew George Parker, we realize how fortunate this pilot was. I'm surprised he didn't shoot the guy and find a ride home some other way!

Two Lions Off One Kill

By Brian Thomas

I have caught about 200 lions for clients and ranchers in Arizona. I do most of my hunting around the Wikieup, Arizona area where I live. These are two stories I thought might be of interest to include in Layne's book.

In December of 1993, a friend of mine by the name of Dave Carlson and I decided to try to catch a lion. I had found where a lion had killed a deer. It rained for 3 days, so we never had a chance to trail this lion. During that time the lion had cleaned up that kill and moved somewhere else.

After the rain let up, we decided to look for a track. We rode up on a place called Muley Mountain, and the dogs found a lion track. It was probably a two-day old track 'cause they couldn't trail it very fast. I let the dogs trail this track, hoping it would get better. After trailing for 3 or 4 miles, they trailed up over a ridge and, on the other side, the dogs found where this lion had killed a yearling calf at the base of a saguaro cactus. The dogs got real excited and ran around trying to figure out where the lion left. Before long they were moving out real fast. They trailed about 2 miles and treed this lion. It was a real nice female lion. Dave shot the lion out of the tree. We were feeling pretty good about the day. Dave got a nice lion, and we killed a calf killer at the same time. When I skinned this lion, I checked her stomach and intestinal track to see what she'd been eating. We expected to find her full of calf meat. This lion didn't have one bit of meat or hair in her anywhere. This really surprised me. We tagged the lion and packed it out to the ranch.

I decided to go back to this kill the next day. Something had fed on that calf and it wasn't the lion we killed, so there had to be another lion in the area. When we got to the kill, the dogs started trailing in the other direction. I could see that the lion had not been back. The calf was exactly like it was the day before. I let the dogs trail for awhile, and I could see a big tom track. The track was two days' old, but they were trailing it fairly well. After they trailed for about 2 miles, they trailed up under some bluffs. We couldn't ride the horse and mule into that country, so we tied them up and went on foot. They finally trailed up on top of the bluffs (these bluffs were about 100 ft. high). We saw the dogs when they jumped this lion out of a crack in the rocks. They bayed this lion right on the edge of this high bluff. This was a nice big male lion. I decided to fill my tag, so I shot this lion. Just as I did, one of my more aggressive dogs got too close to this lion, and he grabbed the dog and put his head in its mouth! I just knew I was going to lose a good dog. But when I shot, the lion fell off the bluff and just before he went over, he dropped the dog. It was a real close call for that red dog.

I wanted to bring this lion out whole because he sure was a big fat lion. It was all Dave and I could do to load him on my mule. I didn't have a scale at the house, so I don't know how much he weighed. But, I measured him before we skinned him out, and he was eight feet, four inches from tip to tip. He was the longest lion I ever caught, so I decided to have him mounted. I caught a larger lion one time, but I never had the opportunity to have him mounted. We'll save that story for another day.

I don't remember exactly what year, but I was working for one of these ranchers up here, working cattle and doing a little lion hunting. I had trailed this lion all day and it was starting to get dark. I decided I would come back the next morning and short cut this lion and try to catch it. I thought I knew where this lion might cross.

The next morning I rode back into this same country, and the dogs hit a running track. All the good dogs just left on the fly. This is good lion country, but hard to get around on horseback. There are only a couple of ways to get thru the country. While I was working my way around (I was riding a young horse), the dogs turned around on the track and flew by me. They figured they were going the wrong way. I rode up on top of the ridge where I could hear. I couldn't hear a single dog. This country has several big canyons and I looked for tracks and listened around, but couldn't tell where the dogs went. These canyons would curve around a lot, so you had to be fairly close to hear the dogs. I was going from canyon to canyon to try to cut some sign or hear something. The colt I was riding was plumb give out. He just couldn't go anymore. So I led the colt out (I don't want to ruin him) and went home. There was nothing else I could do. I came home without a single dog.

The next day I caught a fresh horse and went looking for dogs. It's real hard to find a track in those boulder piles. I rode up on a high point to listen and shoot my gun, hoping the dogs would hear. I hollered until my lungs was about give out. I couldn't find a dog anywhere. I finally went home. One dog showed up that night. I had 8 dogs on this hunt. I wanted to train some pups. The dogs came back one or two a day, and by the end of the week

I had all the dogs back, except 3 good dogs. On the ninth day, I was still looking for dogs. When I got home, a neighboring rancher had called my wife and said he found a fresh calf kill, and hoped I would come to catch this lion. Later that evening the same rancher called and said one of my dogs had showed up at his house (1 of the 3 still missing). So I decided to make a hunt over there and get my dog and maybe catch a lion. That night, when I went out to do the chores, 1 of the missing dogs showed up. All of the dogs were now accounted for except 1. This was the evening of the ninth day.

Day ten. I loaded up all the dogs that could travel and drove over to this other ranch. The rancher had a horse I could ride, so I didn't need a trailer. When I got to the ranch, I found out that a dog I call "Kelly" was the one that showed up at his ranch. She was hungry and sore footed, but she wanted to go hunting. So, I decided to take her.

We rode out to this kill, and the dogs started trailing. We were on this rim and I could hear another dog trailing in the bottom of the canyon. My first thought was someone else is hunting in my area! I wasn't very happy about that. Then I realized that bark sounded familiar. It was my missing dog! All of my dogs were now accounted for! About that time, the other dogs turned down into the canyon and met up with "Bell". Bell was missing for ten days, and when I found her she was trailing a lion!

I know she wasn't trailing a lion for ten days, but she was trailing one now! And, she was on the right end of a big tom track. They went on another quarter of a mile or so and jumped this lion. They had him treed in no time. We shot this calf killer and I loaded Bell on my horse with me. She was so sore and tired and hungry; she was completely give out. Her feet were bleeding and raw. She has a big heart.

This is "big" country and these dogs were not able to get to any ranch houses. These dogs were in the mountains all of this time; Bell for ten days. I had written her off. I was sure glad to see her.

I agree with Layne and Ollie. It is a successful hunt when you get back with all of your dogs in the country we hunt in!

Author's Note: I met Brian thru Chuck Lange. Brian is a good hunter and dog trainer and I am happy to count him among my friends. Like Chuck, he has helped me train dogs and loaned me dogs.

Big male lion caught and photographed by Brian Thomas

Wikieup, Arizona

Big male lion caught by Brian Thomas (right) and 5 good Arizona lion dogs. Accompanied by Bill McBeth.

"I'm sure glad I can jump higher than those hounds! They sure make a lot of noise!"

Caught by Brian Thomas, Wikieup, Arizona

Lion Hunter

Edgar Hyatt

8 November 1974

Come all you rough and tuff hombres
Draw up your chairs to the fire
And we'll make big talk of lion hunting
To see who rates as the biggest liar

Some folks will tell you that running 'em is easy
To hunt them and tree 'em is a snap
But pay them no mind little brother
For that is all a big bunch of crap

I've run them in snow to my pockets
In weather way down below zero
And the first fifty years are the roughest
Then after that you may be a hero

I've run 'em till darkness overtook us
Then make camp on the track for the nite
All you do is build a good fire to keep warm by
And set on your back end and wait for day lite

With nothing to eat not even a biscuit
Before morning your hunger is acute
And you pray the morrow will bring you a favor
And that's let me latch on to that brute

Along about day break come morning
After you have shivered the most of the nite
You make up your mind that dammed certain
That a lion hunter is not to awful bright

Now I'll give you the specifications to hunt lions
To really be called an expert
Well it takes lots of guts and determination
And a number one hat and 44 shirt

And whether you run 'em for money or pleasure
You will find lots of sorrows and joys
And if you live up to the specifications
It will damm sure sort out the men from the boys

I'm sure you will never hear more blessed music
Than old Ranger and Spot and old Red
As they run a hot track down the canyon
With the cougar not to far ahead

Now listen to them old hounds a straining
As each one exerts to get the lead
But now they have stopped their running
I will bet you the chips they have treed

Let's get to them you muscled brained heros
You had better get prepared for a beautiful sight
For the old lion will look down from the tree top
And the old hounds will all want to fight

Well the lion has been treed and slaughtered
This brings to an end the wild chase
As dark settles in your work is not ended
Your ten miles from camp in a hell of a place

The weather is cold as a well digger's fanny
Things don't look to cheerful and bright
The snow is knee deep and crusted
You wonder if you'll ever get home tonight

You drag into the home spread about midnight
You and the dogs are both tired and footsore
And you promise the Good Lord up in Heaven
I'll never hunt lions no more

I've hunted with some of the best of fellows
The most of them true blue to be sure
But once in a while one is chicken
And smells like fresh chicken manure

They tell me of a beautiful place called Heaven
Where nothing is known of sorrow or care
But if they don't have snow to track lions
Why in hell would I want to go there

Now kind folks if you have had time to read this
I hope you got a big kick from the start
Please over look some of the mistakes and language
For this lion hunter is not to damn smart

Some folks think old lion hunters live for ever
Others think they just wither away
But I've always thought they could be about half human
If they're not, why in hell do they smell that way

White Mountain Turkeys

My son, Allen, and I have hunted spring turkeys in the White Mountains of Arizona for the past several years. It is a nice time of the year (most years). This year, April 2001, was an exception. We left home at noon on Thursday and drove to the mountains. It rained all the way to camp. The last ten miles to camp was a dirt road with a lot of clay. We pulled our horse trailer to sleep in. It is not waterproof, but we tied tarps on the sides to keep out the rain. It didn't work and everything we owned got wet. We both slept in the cab of the truck that night (if you can call that sleeping). It rained all that night and until noon the next day. At noon on Friday it started to snow. It quit snowing about mid-afternoon on Friday. I haven't been that miserable since boot camp in Ft. Leonard Wood, MO. The one difference was that I didn't have a pot-bellied sergeant telling me to shine my boots! After it quit snowing, we built a big fire and dried some clothes and bedding so we could get a good night's sleep.

Saturday morning was a cool clear day. We spent the day hunting and scouting. This was the first time we saw Mexican Wolf tracks. They were released back into the wild not far from where we were hunting. A friend of ours saw the wolves.

Saturday evening we split up to listen for turkeys gobbling when they went to roost. We wanted a place to hunt in the morning. We put some birds to bed. However, Allen got turned around and his flashlight quit, and he and I fired our shotguns to locate each other until we finally got back together. That was a real learning experience for Allen (and a frightening one for both of us).

Sunday morning we got up at 3:00 and had coffee and breakfast. At 4:00 we were back where we had heard the turkeys gobble. It was a full moon so we were able to walk without flashlights. When the turkeys started to gobble, about 5:15 (first light), we were right in the middle of them. We had turkeys within 100 yards on both sides of us. We set up and started calling. The turkeys would answer my call on the roost. As soon as they hit the ground they quit talking. There were some coyotes howling near by. That may have been the problem. We walked and called every 100 yards or so. After an hour or so I got a tom to answer my call. Allen and I set up and called again. This gobbler came on the run. He was strutting around looking for a lover. What he got was some BB's from Allen's full choke 12 gauge at 20 yards. A real nice tom!

It was so wet up there that we had to leave our horse trailer and go back for it after the dirt dried out. The trip out of the mountains was a terrible muddy mess. We were lucky to get out. The one ton 4x4 with posi-traction and mud and snow tires had to work hard; we only got stuck once. The first small town we came to we had a good hot meal. I'm sure the waitress wondered where we left our shopping carts and what bridge we were living under! We looked terrible! But we had our gobbler.

Muddy Mess

Allen Brandt with White Mountain Turkey

2001

Arizona Black Bear Hunt

One September, many years ago, Jim Russell, Ron McInnis, and I made a trip to Central Arizona to hunt Black bear.

Early in the morning I heard Ron or Jim shoot. I was a ways off, so I made my way over there to see what had happened. Ron had wounded a bear. We all started looking for it. I made a circle, looking for any blood trails. I found a spot of blood on an old cow trail. It was a hard trail to follow, and I was trailing along like an old hound with my eyes glued to the ground. It suddenly dawned on me that there was no more blood. I heard a noise behind me. I added 2+2 and came up with 4 real pronto! I swung around and the bear was right behind me standing on his hind legs. I shot from the hip and dropped the bear in his tracks. It wasn't a very big bear but he was big enough to hurt or kill me, which is exactly what he planned to do. When he fell I could touch him with my gun barrel!

I made a bear rug out of him and I hung him in my trophy room.

I enjoyed hunting with Ron and Jim. On another bear hunt Ron and I made one day, Ron killed a record book bear. That was on the San Carlos Apache Indian Reservation. Ron and I used to hunt there a lot. We used to pay $25.00 for a season-long bear tag over the counter. Times are sure changing. There are too many people in Arizona now, and the Indians charge too much for hunting on their reservations.

The Lee Brothers

A friend of mine, Lewie Hughes, and I decided to make a deer hunt up in the White Mountains of Arizona in the early '70's. He was managing a feed yard for F.I.C.O. at the time. When Lewie came to pick me up, he had a black eye and a swollen lip. I asked, "What the hell happened, Lewie?" "Oh," he said. "These damn cowboys - you can't win. I have to get on my knees and beg them to come to work, then I have to fight them to get them to leave." He was sure upset.

We drove to the Blue River area of the White Mountains and set up camp and tied up the horses. The next day we rode out early looking for deer. (This was back in the days when there was some good deer hunting in Northern Arizona. There are very few deer left. Lots of elk.) We hobbled our horses and made a morning hunt on foot.

When we got back to where we left the horses, they were gone. We could see the tracks where a big bear came through and spooked the horses. They were easy to trail and we found them a mile or so away. On the way back to camp, we rode through a small pasture. When we were just about to the other end of the pasture, we saw a horse coming on the run. Lewie figured it out muy pronto. "Make a run for the gate and don't let this stud take your mare!" We made a mad dash for the gate. It was a close call! Lewie saved the day. I wouldn't have figured it out that quick.

That evening we drove to Clell Lee's ranch. Lewie knew Clell pretty well. We had a nice visit. I really enjoyed seeing his jaguar hides and other trophies. After dinner, Lewie and Clell went out to the barn to look at a horse. I stayed behind and drank coffee with his wife. I commented how jealous I was of Clell's hunting. She exclaimed, "That's all Clell ever wanted to do. I can never get him to help on the ranch."

She told me the story about the time she needed to round up the cattle. She told Clell she would go up to the line shack a few miles up the canyon and get things ready. The plan was for Clell to come up and help the following day. Clell decided to take a few hounds along and exercise some dogs along the way. As luck would have it, they found a lion track, and Clell was a day late getting up to the line shack.

Those Lee Brothers definitely had their priorities straight in my book!

Many years after that, Ollie and I visited with Dale Lee in Tucson. He was a great old man with great stories to tell. He had a bronze in his house with a lion treed in a saguaro cactus. He claimed he only ever caught one in a saguaro. I can't imagine how. I asked Dale if he thought there were more lions now than when he was hunting. (This was probably a year before he died.) He told me that, in his opinion, there are more lions now than in the '50's, '60's, and '70's when he and his brothers did so much hunting. The main reason was the fact that the government doesn't pay to hunt lions anymore and sport hunters are fewer now.

I enjoyed visiting with Clell and Dale very much. They probably forgot more about lion hunting than most people will ever know. Dale Lee's book, "Life of the Greatest Guide", is one of the better hunting books that I've read.

A Covey of Lions

By Chuck Lange

I have guided for lions and other big game in the Northwest area of Arizona for a long time. So far I have caught about a hundred lions for clients and ranchers.

A friend of mine, Mike Swift, came over from California to do some hunting and train some dogs. We caught a lion on the Kane Springs Ranch one day, and the next day we decided to move camp and hunt on the SV Ranch not far from there.

It was in the winter and the ground was frozen solid. We had about eight dogs between us on this hunt. We were only about a mile from camp when the dogs hit a real good lion track. I jumped off my horse, but the ground was frozen so hard I couldn't find a track. All we could do was hope the dogs were going the right way. They trailed for about 2 miles and when we caught up with them, they had the lion caught. It was a female lion and she was on a small rock pile, and all the dogs were barking treed. We rode out on this ridge to where this lion was, and before we got close to her, she bailed off the rock pile. We watched her cross the canyon and climb out on the other side. This canyon was a steep rocky canyon, and we were high enough we could see everything. This lion made a loop to the right and crossed the canyon again. She jumped up on a rock and watched all of the dogs go by, one by one. When she thought all the dogs were past, she jumped off the rock and started back on her back track exactly the way she just came. We knew then we were watching a lion that had been caught before. We were really enjoying the show. The only thing that ruined it for this lion was that Mike had one old dog that was way behind. He was sore footed and not barking, just trailing up the other dogs. This old dog and that lion met face to face on her back track. When that old dog came nose to nose with this lion, he let out a bawl. The other dogs were trying to figure out where this lion was, so when they heard this old dog bark, they ran up there to help. This lion ran and climbed back up on the same rock pile she just left from! We decided at that point we better hurry and kill this lion before she wears the dogs out and out smarts them and gets away. So, I took my pistol and started down to shoot her, and she bailed out again! This time she went down the canyon about two hundred yards and climbed out on the other side where she was when she watched all the dogs go by. Then she made another small loop and went back to the bottom of the canyon. The dogs were running around trying to figure out where she went. She made so many tracks and so many loops in that canyon, there was lion scent everywhere. After she sat in the bottom of the canyon and watched the dogs for awhile, she started up the side of the canyon we were on. That's when we lost sight of her. Up until that time we got to watch the whole show.

I walked down into this canyon a ways to see if I could help the dogs or shoot the lion or something. I was only about fifty yards from the top of the ridge when all of a sudden I saw the lion walking towards me! When she saw me, she whirled and ran out of sight. I ran up the hill and called the dogs. The dogs came to me and I put them on the track, and they caught her again in a small rock pile. She jumped again before I could get a shot and ran back to the original rock pile where they caught her the first time! Before I could get close enough to shoot, she jumped again! This time she stayed on the same side of the canyon we were on. The dogs trailed her up into some small bluffs and lost the track. Apparently this lion made another loop down there to throw the dogs off like she'd been doing. I was slipping around to where I could see and maybe spot the lion running down the canyon when something caught my eye.

There was this lion about ten feet directly below me hiding in the rocks. This time I shot the lion and the hunt was over. That was one smart, cagey lion. The whole hunt only lasted a couple of hours, but those dogs got a work out and some experience on that hunt!

A few years ago my brother-in-law, Jay Runston, was running the Windmill Ranch not far from here. He was having some serious problems with lions killing calves. I decided to make a hunt down there and see what I could find. Trout Creek runs through this ranch, and it is a real rough canyon. In a ten mile stretch, there are only two or three places you can cross on horseback. But, it is good lion country.

It was in November when I started hunting on that ranch. The first day out we hit a lion track at a place we called Bull Springs. The dogs trailed this lion off the mountain for about three quarters of a mile, when I heard them jump the lion. They trailed that jumped lion as fast as they could go all the rest of the day and could never catch the damned thing! They never traveled any long distance. They just trailed around in the same general area. If I hadn't seen the lion track myself, I would have thought they were running a fox or something. I finally called off the dogs and went home. I decided I would get some fresh dogs and come back in the morning. I had four dogs on this hunt, and I had two fresh dogs at home.

I went back the second day with all six dogs. The same thing happened the second day. This lion wouldn't leave this piece of country. My guess was that she had kittens. Any other lion would have left the country, or treed, or something. This was very unusual. After they ran this lion for awhile, they trailed through a big patch of cholla cactus. The dogs were full of cactus, so I pulled them off the track and pulled out as much cactus as I could and went home. When I got home I called a friend, John Hunt, who has some good dogs, and asked if he'd help me catch this lion.

The third day John and I hunted this same country, but we couldn't find a good track.

The fourth day, Thanksgiving Day, Jay and I decided to have a look around. I promised my family I would be home by 11:00 a.m. However, I knew the dogs would determine when we got home.

We rode down in to Trout Creek Canyon to look around and see if we could find a place to set a trap and catch this calf killer. I took all six of my dogs along in case we found a good track. While we were looking for a place to set a trap, we found a place in the fence that needed repair. While we were fixing the fence, the dogs found a lion track up one of the draws. It was a pretty good track. We had to hurry 'cause it was a long ways to rim out and get to the gate to catch up with the dogs. They were really moving this track. Jay commented several times that he thought he saw more than one lion track. But, it was hard to tell with all the dog tracks.

At about 4:00 p.m. Jay said he would go back to get the truck and trailer and meet me up ahead at Salt Creek. We knew we were going to get our asses ate out for being late. But I just had a hunch we were going to catch this lion.

Right at dusk I was ready to call off the hunt. The deal was: if I caught the lion, I would build a big fire and Jay would come to me. The dogs trailed off into a steep side canyon and up on the other side. There were a half a dozen or so of those Palo Cristi trees close together. I was just about to call the dogs off when they trailed up under one of the Palo Cristi trees. All of a sudden, four lions ran out from underneath this tree! A female with three cubs! They scattered like a covey of quail! The dogs treed one kitten and caught one on the ground and killed it. The female ran past me, not ten yards away! I didn't have time to get my rifle out of the scabbard. The female and one kitten got away, and I shot the kitten that was treed.

My dogs were so give out and their feet so sore, I couldn't hunt them for two weeks. I never went back after that female.

I don't remember what time I had Thanksgiving dinner that night, but I do remember getting some hot tongue and cold shoulder!

Author's Note: Chuck and I have partnered on cattle and have been friends for many years. He and I enjoy swapping lion hunting stories and visiting every chance we get. He is a good hunter and a good friend. He has also helped me train pups and loaned me dogs.

Chuck Lange with female lion.

Male lion and "good dogs".
Caught and photographed by Chuck Lange.

Alaska Grizzly Bear

In the 1980's when my brother, Dale, was living in Juneau, Alaska, Dad and I made a hunt up there for a Grizzly bear. We flew commercial to Juneau, then Dale had a friend take us out to Admiralty Island in a small boat. We stayed in a forest service cabin close to shore.

It was in May and the bears were just coming out of hibernation. The only food source I could see was a native grass growing between the seashore and the timber. There was a 20-foot strip of lush grass all along the shore. We would leave our camp early and get the wind in our face. As we would walk slowly along the shore, we would glass for bears feeding on the grass.

On the second day of our trip we located a bear. We slipped around until we got about 200 yards from this bear. Dale and I laid down and got a good rest on a dead log. I had read a lot about Grizzly hunting. The best way to kill one is to break them down in the shoulder or back so that they don't hurt or kill you. Dale aimed for the bear's back, and I aimed for the front shoulder and on the count of three we both fired. I was shooting a .338 magnum and Dale was shooting a .375. We both hit where we were aiming. The bear could not go anywhere. He threw a hell of a fit, but he didn't last long.

He was about a 500 lb. bear. He stunk terrible and it was a miserable job skinning him.

On the way back to camp we saw a large female bear with two half grown cubs. We went to camp and we got Dad. Then we sneaked over to where these bears were and we took some pictures. We took our rifles in case we needed them for self-defense. We were very careful not to get between the sow and the cubs. Dad really enjoyed watching them. For some reason the pictures didn't come out. I think the camera broke or something. Yet, the memories are still very clear in our minds.

That was the only bear we shot on that trip. It was my first trip to Alaska. It is a beautiful state for a Southern Arizona rat like myself. The amount of water in that country is a sight for sore eyes. We should run a pipeline from Alaska to Arizona!

I had the bear hide tanned and I gave it to my twin cousins, Dave and Dan Weirsma in Apple Valley, California. They have a Silversmith shop there and they have the bear rug displayed in their shop.

Otto and Dale Brandt with Alaskan Grizzly.

Fly In Fishing

In the 90's, Eileen, Allen and I made two fishing trips up North.

The first was to Admiralty Island off the coast of Juneau, Alaska. We flew commercial to Juneau where we met my brother, Dale, and his wife, Doreen. Dale and Doreen were living in Juneau at that time. In Juneau we bought supplies and fishing gear and chartered a single-engine plane (Beaver) on floats to fly us to Alexander Lake on Admiralty Island. This Beaver was an old plane, built, I think, in the mid to late '50's. It was beautifully restored in every detail. I had never been in a plane on floats, so this was a real treat for me. It had a radial engine and, on take off, made a lot of noise. The airplane had a G.P.S. (Global Positioning System) on board and the pilot entered the latitude and longitude for the Lake and we were on our way.

The trip was only about 45 minutes long. After the pilot leveled off, I started to quiz him about the airplane. He could tell by my questions that I was a pilot. He pushed a button on the steering yoke column and moved the column and yoke over to me. "Go ahead and fly", he said. I took the controls, but I wasn't all that interested in flying, although it would have been fun to learn to take off and land in the water. I reluctantly took the controls. I was spending more time enjoying the scenery than I was flying. Suddenly I spotted a grizzly bear fishing in a stream. I decided to go down and have a closer look. The pilot pushed the button on the control column and returned it to the pilot's position. "We are not looking for bear, we are going to Alexander Lake", he exclaimed. Some people just don't know how to have fun!

The landing at the Lake was perfect. We taxied to the shore and unloaded our supplies. When that plane took off, we were on vacation. No phones, no faxes, no computers, no people, and no problems (we hoped).

The Forest Service cabin was great. Bunk beds, potbellied stove, cut firewood, and an outhouse (not Eileen's favorite amenity). Allen, of course, was not interested in unpacking. He was ready to go fishing.

This Lake was probably 200 acres in size, and we had the only cabin on the Lake. It even came with a row boat and oars. Life is good. So was the fishing. One of the few places I've been where you have to hide behind a tree to bait your hook! We caught several different species of trout in the Lake. Fresh trout for dinner, cooked on an open fire. I love fish that doesn't taste like fish.

The next day we packed our backpacks and followed a well-marked trail to the ocean. There we found a stream with spawning salmon. They were not too interested in our lures (which is normal), but we did catch a few (and snagged a few). We filleted the salmon for the 2 hour walk back to the cabin. Salmon for dinner tonight.

After several days, the pilot showed up right on time. He didn't offer to let me fly again!

I strongly recommend this kind of vacation for anyone experiencing stress. It was great fun.

The second trip we made was to Lake Tusunia in British Columbia, Canada, a year later. We flew the company's C182 to the Seattle area where the girls were living. After a nice visit, it was off to B. C. The transponder quit working on the way to Seattle, so we had to stay clear of the Seattle and Vancouver T.C.A.'s (Terminal Control Areas). The weather was typical Northwest weather – low clouds, fog, etc. I was not an instrument certified pilot, so I hired a pilot in the Seattle area to help me. I didn't need to get into a jackpot up there.

We flew to Victory Island to clear Customs. I was familiar with flying into Mexico, so I had enough papers to choke a horse. Whatever they could possibly want, I had it. I taxied to the Customs ramp, took my armload of papers and walked to the Customs office. The ole boy said, "Where ya headed?" I told him and started to hand him the papers. "Good luck fishing. Call me on this frequency when you come back." Man, this was a piece of cake compared to Mexico. Didn't even have to pay a bribe!

We programmed the G.P.S. for the lake and we were off. I was flying, Eileen and Allen were in the back seats, and the hired pilot was doing the navigating. I could see a lot of low clouds in the Vancouver area, so I climbed on top at about 10,000'. I thought I was wasting my money by hiring this IFR pilot. About that time Vancouver approach called me and asked me what our flight conditions were. I told him we were VFR on top. He informed me that was not permissible in Canada. I replied, "O.K., then hand us off to Center and we will file an IFR flight plan." He explained that was not permissible in Canada either. We needed to file an IFR plan on the ground. Damn! Maybe I do like Mexico better! I consulted with my IFR pilot. He said, "Let's stay VFR and descend below the clouds and we'll just do some scud running." I agreed, and down we went. We proceeded on our way. The clouds kept getting lower and lower. Finally, we were flying in what they call a fiord. It was like flying inside of a tunnel. Clouds above, canyon walls on both sides and water below. I was praying the engine wouldn't quit. My hired pilot kept looking at the map and looking outside, and he was beginning to make me nervous. I knew if we ever made a wrong turn up one of these fiords we could be in serious trouble. I asked him if he was absolutely sure where we were. He pointed to his map and said "We are right here. Turn right at the next fork in the canyon and there will be an old gold mine about ¼ mile." We made the turn, and, sure enough, there it was. I was feeling much better about the situation. After a few more miles we began to see a long ridge with about ¼ of a mile of daylight between the ridge and the clouds. We climbed out of the canyon and over the ridge. From there we could see the lodge. My pilot asked, "Can you land on that dirt strip?" I informed him we based our airplane at a shorter strip than that. He said, "There have been a lot of plane wrecks here." I told him for damned sure we wouldn't be among them. After landing, I sent my pilot to Seattle with the airplane and instructed him when to pick us up.

The lodge and cabins were #1. The fishing was better. We caught our limit of Lake Trout early every day and had them smoked in their smoker. It was some of the best fish I have ever eaten.

One afternoon I hiked down the canyon to examine their homemade hydropower generator. It was a mechanical marvel. Gil Smith would have been impressed.

At the appointed hour, we heard the familiar whine of a great Cessna 182. The pilot was on time and the flight to Seattle was uneventful with good weather.

The Customs guy treated us real good. I don't know if the bag of smoked trout helped or not. It sure didn't hurt. Greased political wheels always turn easier.

On the way back to Arizona, I couldn't get over the millions of acres of timber. It is a shame that the environmentalist extremists have become as powerful as they are. We are all environmentalists. No one wants to destroy our forests. We all want to maintain a balance. But humans need to be part of the equation. There is no good reason why our forests can't be viable and productive. Shutting down all those sawmills and related industries is crazy. We need to fix that. I wasn't surprised when I saw a huge sign where we fueled in Boise, Idaho that said "Clinton Free Zone".

I've always been more of a hunter than a fisherman, but I truly enjoyed those fishing trips. I just enjoy the outdoors and observing how other people do things and how they think.

I have people ask me all the time, "Where is there a good place to go fishing in Arizona?" I tell them there aren't any good places in Arizona. Alaska and Canada will spoil a person from fishing anywhere else.

Eileen Brandt fishing on Admiralty Island, Alaska.

New Mexico Stories

The following stories were transcribed from a cassette tape owned by Ollie Barney. The storyteller is unknown to us. I have tried unsuccessfully to find out who he is. All I know is he was a government hunter in New Mexico, probably in the 1940's and 1950's. He is a great storyteller. Enjoy...

Bloodhound Pup

I had been to work for the U.S. Wildlife Service only a short time until I realized what a hunter and a trapper sure did need was a good kind of trail dog. A dog you can put on the track of something and he will stay with it. And, I would need a dog I could manage and call back when I needed to. I didn't need an old dog that would look for the county line. Then I would spend all of my time a-looking for him.

I come home one day with a little old Bloodhound pup in the palm of one hand. Just a bundle of wrinkles. He was so young he didn't even have his eyes open, and he was so weak he couldn't hold his mouth shut. And, my wife took one look at that little ole sorry lookin' thing and said "Now what are you going to do with that blame thing?" I said, "I guess we will just let the poor little motherless son-of-a-bitch die, just like the rest of his brothers and sisters!" Well, the woman in her come to the top. She sent one kid in one direction and another kid in the other direction to get some sweet milk and Karo syrup. And, she took a washcloth and was a-squeezing that mixture into the corner of his mouth and rubbin' his throat and gettin' him to swaller. Now to say the least, that dog lived. And she was the only mother that he could remember. In that dog's book that woman turned out to be his God. I didn't see anything wrong with that, in my book anyway.

Well, I'm trying to get me a little start with some better dogs. Now I've had my baptism with them other kind. You know, their daddy was a trailin' man and, among other things, their mother was a lady about town. Now I started that ole pup as early as you could start a dog. I hauled him up there in the front seat with me. I made a buddy out of 'im. Well, he finally got too big for that, ya know, 4-5 months old, and he wanted to spend most of his time lookin' out of my winder anyway. So, I'm jist a-makin' him ride in the back where he belonged. I'll show him his place.

I was a lookin' over this area between the Stewart Hall's Ranch and the Red River Ranch there at Springer, New Mexico for it was a real good place for those old mama coyotes to make a den when it come time to have their puppies. And, it was a-gittin' that time. I stopped out there about a half a mile and I'm a-runnin' the telescope sight of my rifle over that area, and I thought I seen a coyote pass over a ridge and lay down in some grass. So I'm a-takin' my time and I'm a-goin' along there slow and when I got pretty close to that area where that coyote either went over that ridge or laid down, there was a little spring down in the draw there that furnished water for that area and it supplied water for most of the wildlife in that area. And, this ole Bloodhound pup, ya know, has got his feet up on the side of my pickup and he was a-runnin' his ole radar nose back and forth and directly he just woofed, ya know, and run to the back of my truck. Well, I just stopped. Well, he jumped out and started up that little ridge. He hadn't took 30 steps when an ole coyote just raised up out of that grass and started walking down towards that little spring in that draw. Well, I realized right then what that ole mama coyote was a-doin' to my Bloodhound pup. She was a-leadin' him into a trap. Now most of the coyotes that he'd a-seen up til then had a trap on their foot and a couple of old dogs to do the hard work. But he was a-gettin' big enough and hard headed enough to think that he could handle jist about most any situation, and he just took to that ole mama coyote. Well, she let him git pretty close. Then she just broke into a little easy run and faded down over the bank toward that little spring. Well now, while that's a-happening, this cowboy's not standin' still. I'm out of my pickup and down on one knee and I've got that telescope on that rifle lined up and I'm ready to do business 'cause I knew it was a-fixin' to pick up.

Well, sure enough, that ole daddy coyote was a-layin' there in the shade, and they brought my Bloodhound pup out a-there. One of them ole coyotes would run up behind him and grab him by the seat of his britches, tear a chunk out of it, turn him around and go right on by. Well, he'd turn around to fight and sit on that thing to defend that position. Well, the other coyote would come by on the other side and git him by the hip pocket and go the other way. Now him a-tryin' to sit on that thing and tryin' to fight and tryin' to git back to me....now, that woulda bin funny if that woulda bin anybody else's dog but mine! Now that ain't a-suitin' me, not one bit! Now I've got that telescope sight lined up and I'm ready to do business. Well that ole mama coyote widened out there about 10 foot and give me that room. Well I let the wind out of her. Well, at the crash of that rifle, that old daddy coyote just looked up like he never had noticed me before. Well, I'm busy a-fannin' the bolt on that rifle and before he made up his mind what was a-happenin', he didn't live to regret his mistake either. Now I was amazed at the courage my Bloodhound pup recovered, especially when he found out that them coyotes was plumb dead. He'd go over and shake one for awhile and then he'd go over and shake the other one. Now he showed them fellers how ta play rough! Now that was the makin' of my Bloodhound pup. That's the first time I've saved his life, but it wasn't the only time that we've saved one another's life over a long period of years!

Dog Theft

One day Bruce Bull and I made a trip to Taos to pick up some sacks for my combine. We no sooner got to town when Bruce spotted this dog.

Bruce says "Pull over. Pull over there. Wait a minute. I found my dog." Well, I whipped it over to the curb, you know, and stopped and there was a great big, prettiest, red dog. Looked like a bird dog of some kind - sure looked like a good 'un. Bruce whistled at him and said, "Com'ere Red. What're you doin?". And that old dog came just as straight to Bruce as he could come. Bruce got him by the collar and pulled him up on the floor boards and he shut the door. "Well" he said, "Come on. I found my dog."

Well, we pulled out of town there probably a couple of miles and that old dog kept a-tryin to look out, but Bruce wouldn't let 'im. And I thought it was a little bit odd, but, well, that's his dog, he'll do what he wants to with him, I guess. 'Rectly Bruce reached down and he unbuckled the collar on that dog. Held it up - it had some tags and identifications looked like of some kind. Bruce said, "San Bernardino, Califorry." "Ah" he said, "I don't guess we're gonna need that thing." and he just sailed that dog collar right out that winder. Well I realized right then what I was a party to. We had stole that dog right there in the middle of Taos, New Mexico in broad open day light and me a-drivin' a government pickup. And, I said, "Bruce, my Gawd a'mighty. If anything ever comes of this I never will get through makin' out reports on it before they run me plumb off." And, I said, "What'll be a whole lot worse than that, some old boy'll a-come whizzin' up behind us with a 2-roll shotgun and nail both of us to the side of this dad-blamed mountain." Bruce said, "Ah, I don't think anything'll come of it." Said, "I bin a-watchin' that ole dog for 4 or 5 days. Some tourist come around here, you know, let that ole dog out to go to the bathroom and while they was a-rubberneckin' around over these curio shops that old dog probably got to followin' one of these Indians around and wonderin' whether he needed to stay or point him. They couldn't find their dog and they just finally had to go off and leave him. Now, if he follers one of these Indians home and it comes a bad winter, that Indian'll probably wind up eatin' that dog." He said, "Now, I won't do that to him."

Well, that settled that argument as far as I was concerned.

...And Airedales

...and, I said, "Bruce, I need an Airedale dog. I'm gonna have to get me a start of Airedales. You know them Bloodhounds won't stop an old killer bear. That Bloodhound'll get about so close to that ole bear and he'll go to doing missionary work. He'd rather anybody get scratched but him. But now that Airedale is another piece of furniture, that's what I understand." He said, "You are so right!"

He said, "I've got an Airedale right here at the house and I'll give him to you under one condition. If he ain't no talent you promise me you'll get rid of him. Now, the only thing I know about that old dog - he will fight. These hounds of mine thought they was gonna run that old dog off when he come to my place here a couple of months ago. He just backed up against a tree and he whooped every one of my dogs that come to him. You know, that old dog was so poor and weak that he was just a-tremblin'. I felt so sorry for him so I went to feedin' him and I hoped to find him a good home." "But," he said, "now you promise you'll get rid of him if he ain't no account." Well, I promised him I would.

I said, "What do you call this old dog?" He said, "I don't know. I've called him everything I can think of and he don't answer to nothing. Maybe you know some cuss words that I don't. I can't even get that old dog's attention." I said, "Well, how about we jus call him 'Rags'." "Yeah" he said. "a wrung out one". We kinda laughed about it and I carried him home.

Well, a rancher there at Miami, New Mexico had given me a female Airedale dog that had bit about half the school kids there was in that area and he was afraid he'd wind up in a lawsuit or somethin'. And he got after me to take that dog off of his hands. I thought that was a pretty good kind of deal. I didn't find her mean to bite or anything. All she wanted you to do was just leave her alone.

Well, I took her home and tied her to the bottom of a little apple tree with about 20 foot of chain so she could reach the back door of my garage and the side door, too. I thought she might be the answer to some of my problems. About every three months an armload of my traps would walk out of my garage.

Well, there one night about 11 o'clock - 11:30 - hell, about the time the little local bar closed, I heard old Pat hit the end of her chain and kinda woof and bark and somebody hollered. And, I heard the footsteps goin' down that alley...pitty-pat, pitty-pat, pitty-pat...and went right on out of hearing. And, I thought, buddy, you better get out there and see what took place. I turned on the porch light and I got out there, and old Pat was still a-worrin' what was left of a sleeve of a Levi jacket - just about from the elbow down. Well, you know, I never lost another trap. They was sure enough afraid to walk out of that garage past that Airedale dog.

A Boy and His Dog

Now, the first crop of puppies that I got out of old Pat and old Rags - well, them was the prettiest little fellers you'd ever looked at. Old Pat was real cranky about them puppies. Man, just the slightest provocation she'd show you every tooth she had, and I stayed out of that old gal's way. But I had a little old cotton-headed kid that wasn't old enough to go to school. And, it looked like he was a privileged character around that dog pen. He just come and went like he dad-blamed well pleased.

And, he came in there one day with the runt of them little old Airedale pups. He said, "Daddy, this little feller ain't got no place to nurse." Said "Pat had 8 puppies and she's just got 7 places." He said, "When I pull one of them old big pups a-loose and give this one a little bit of a drink that old big pup will go to squealing in a little bit and old Pat will go to lookin' at me. I've got to let that old big pup go back." Said, "Now if this little feller don't get something to eat, he's a-gonna die." Well, now we'd raised a Bloodhound pup on a baby bottle and we'd raised a bobcat kitten on a doll bottle. Well, we may just as well try to raise an Airedale.

Well, that little ole dog lived and when she got big enough she lived with that boy. She made every track that that young 'un made. She thought wherever he was that was where she belonged and that female was so hard to convince. Now that kid of mine would be playin' up and down the alley, backyard, wherever with them little Mexican boys and once in a while a little argument would break out and he'd wind up on the bottom. It seems like there was a whole lot more of them little Mexican boys than there was little tow-headed gringos. Well, when her partner went to making one kind of noises, old sis would just sit out there and watch the fun. But, when her partner went to makin' the wrong kind of noise, it was a gittin' the time for her. She'd get somebody by the hind leg and she'd start pulling them off. She would even up the odds for her partner. Now, that little old dog never did start any of them arguments, but she dad-blamed wound up several of them.

Hurley had an old tennis ball and he'd bounce that thing against the side of the garage hour after hour after his brothers had already gone to school, and if that ball hit one of them slats that was patching a crack in that garage and it run off out in the alley or out on the lawn, that little ole dog would go git that ball and bring it back to him.

Well, when it come summertime, in order for the kids to have a little something to do - they wasn't big enough, you know, to find a job somewhere - the high school coach managed for an old drag from somewhere and I had a Government pickup and a great long tow chain. Well, we took that little ole drag and I drug the weeds off of 8 or 10 big ole lots there that laid Southwest of where I lived, and we burnt the weeds, the kids picked up the rocks and I hauled 'em off. And the sheep ranchers around there gave me enough of that ole junk net wire to make a backstop. And, I moonlight requisitioned enough long poles off of the U.S. Forest to put up that backstop, and that coach managed for enough old busted bats with tape all over 'em. Now we're just a-playin' with old rag balls so they won't have to have any gloves. Well, maybe the catcher and the first baseman... Well, the two biggest boys would, you know, start choosin' up sides and it'd finally trickle down to the little bitty boys and maybe some of the little girls that wanted to play. Most of 'em wanted to stand on the sidelines and giggle, you know, and stick their finger in the corner of their mouth. Well, anyhow when it got to them little 'uns you had to toss that ball underhanded to 'em. Well, this kid of mine would be a-playin', you know, and that little Airedale dog would be a-floatin' around out there in the infield with the rest of the kids' dogs. Looked like everybody had several of 'em. Well, we had to call time out once in a while to watch them little dogs fight. Now that little ole Airedale thought it was a lot of fun to fight, but it was a whole lot more fun to win! She'd get one of them old cur dogs by the front foot and go to shakin' on it and chewin' on it, and it wasn't gonna be very long before that dog was ready to go home.

Well, if this kid of mine ever, ever hit that ball that Airedale would beat somebody to it and she'd start home with that ball. She could make a home run. Well, whoever grabbed that Airedale dog and took that ball away from her was the one that got bit.

And, while he's a-holdin' that bit place, she'd grab that ball again and take it on home. Well, they had to have a meetin' and change the rules. If he played ball they had to tie that dad-blamed dog up at the house. Well, now, that was understandable. But that tying that dog up turned out to be a problem. You didn't tie her up by the collar. She'd pull back till she was unconscious. I've undone her a number of times and pumped the wind back into that little ole hard-headed female. Well, I made a harness for her so I could snap her up with a chain. You didn't tie her up with a strap or a rope. In just a little bit she'd come a-trailin' that thing back out on the baseball field. And, you wonder why I didn't put her in the pen and git it over with. That dad-blamed Airedale would climb that there net wire fence just like it was a ladder and she'd just fall out the back side, and she'd be a-standing at your feet when you opened the back door. One time we had that Airedale dog tied up during the baseball game. Them little Mexican boys thought now here's a good chance for us to take up a little bit of the slack. And that gringo kid wound up on the bottom and he didn't have a dog. But he did have a brother a-playin' out there that was older than he was. This brother walked over to that old pile of taped up bats, you know, selected one of them and went over to home plate. And, he tapped it on the home plate 2 or 3 times and he walked over to that little fight and he took his battin' practice <u>right</u> there. Well, that almost broke up the Wagon Mound All Star Dirty Socks baseball team - well, them that had socks. Well, that's what the kids wanted to name it and, if they did, that was good enough for me.

 Well, next year when it came time for that cotton-headed kid to go to school, we had another problem with that Airedale dog. If he went to school, she was going to have to stay at the house. Well, we couldn't get her to understand that part. We'd snap her up with a chain while that kid went to school. Well, after an hour or two, there when his mama got tired of listenin' to that dad-blamed dog have one fit right after another, she'd go out there and unsnap that dog. That Airedale would trail that kid to the schoolhouse and the first person that went in or out of that schoolhouse, that Airedale went between their feet and she went to lookin' for that young 'un. Well, most of them kids there knowed that Airedale already from the baseball days. And, when they got ready to put that dog out of that schoolhouse, they better be ready to look up that little ole tow-headed young 'un and let him do it. Well, he brought her home a number of times 'cause they got tired of gettin' bit, and I was probably lucky I didn't wind up in a lawsuit also. Well, when that kid'd get out of school, you know, that little ole Airedale'd a-sit out there on that rock fence hour after hour a-waitin' for that kid to come around the corner about 2 blocks away. And, when he showed up, here went that Airedale. Now, don't let nobody, anybody else's dog either, get between her and her partner til they got their congratulations over with. Well, so much for an Airedale dog and her God.

Bear Huntin' New Mexico Style

It was opening day of early bear season where you can run bear with dogs if you want to, and I've got a little string of traps up the Awahee Canyon on that McDaniels Ranch. They had planted some wild turkey and other exotic birds in that area and I'm a-tryin' to hold the bobcat and coyotes off of 'em and give them turkeys a little better start. And, I'm just like them other government hunters...I'm a day late and a dollar short. So, I'm pickin' up my trap line just as early as I can, and I had all them traps took up but about 4. And, directly I heard the runnin' and the shootin' and the hollerin' and the raisin' of the Devil up on that Big Miami mesa. And I thought now them cowboys have done jumped theirselves a bear. They probably knowed where them bears was a runnin' all the time anyways. Now in a minute I heard rocks a-tinklin' on that old rock slide.

Now I'd looked at that thing a number of times and just wondered if the right rock, or maybe the wrong one, whichever comes first, got pulled a-loose there at the bottom, how much of that loggin road it would cover up or how many pickups it would tear up. So, I just set tight right where I was and in just a little bit an ole mama bear and a yearlin' cub come a-floatin across that road in front of my pickup. Their tongues was out and they was a-slobberin', and that old mama bear was so poor that her old belly flopped just like a wagon sheet. Well, I'm haulin' a young Airedale and a young Bloodhound, and I'm just tryin' to get them old pups so as I can manage 'em. I've got to have a dog that's under control. I don't need an old dog that runs off half the time and then spend the other half of the time a-lookin' for 'em. Them pups seen that ole bear and really put up a holler. Oh, they wanted some of that bear business! Well, I knew that they didn't need any of that kind of bear business. 'Cause I knew if they took a-holt of that bear that ole mama bear might kill one or maybe both of them pups, and I wasn't ready to kill a bear right then....I didn't think anyway. And, in just a little bit the brother to the first cub came floatin' across the road and he was a-slobberin, and those pups sure did put up a holler that time. Well, I'm a-gittin' a little bit enthused myself. That ole mama bear was a-takin' that other cub and a-goin' on. I seen her top out over there on a little game trail on the west rim and they was still a-hoofin' it. Now I thought this might be a chance to train on my young dogs a little, so I just unbuckled the leashes on my pups and said "Go git 'em!".

Now, that Bloodhound run up behind that young bear and grabbed him by the back foot and just run right over the top of that bear; he just turned him a cartwheel. When that young bear started squealin' and a-bawlin' that Bloodhound thought of some worrying and he better git back home and start tendin' to it. He come a-whizzin' back down that loggin' road and almost slid by my pickup before he managed to go under it. It looked like a whole lot better place to him.

Now, this Airedale family of dogs is another piece of furniture. When an Airedale gets close enough to a bear to get a good look at 'im, the next thing they want to do is to taste of 'im. And, if they live over it, they'll bite 'im again. But that Bloodhound family had rather anybody get scratched but him. Now that Airedale waltzed up to that young bear and got him by the jaw. He just froze to 'im, and around and around they went. That Airedale was a-stickin' out just like the tail of a kite. Now that Bloodhound thought the Airedale looked like he needed some help. So he came out from under that pickup. Oh, he sounded brave. He made a lot of noise. That bear swung that Airedale around and hit that pup with her. That hound pup thought "My God Almighty I've done been got again!". And under my truck he went again. Now I was beginnin' to have some thoughts about just what kind of a bear dog is my Bloodhound a-gonna make?

Now directly that bear raked that Airedale loose from its jaw and he slapped her across that loggin' road about 4 turns. I'm beginning to wonder whether I'm a-goin to take an Airedale home with me. Then that little bear went up a tree there next to the cut bank. Then I went over to my Airedale to see what kind of patching up job I was a-gonna have to do, or if I was gonna have to do a funeral. Well, it didn't appear like there was anything wrong with that little lady that was hurt except her pride. She dad-blamed near bit me for my trouble. Now that little lady was still full of fight.

Now I looked up and down this canyon and I seen a place where I might be able to climb out. I thought I would climb out of this canyon and find me a rock and knock that little bear out of that tree to do some more trainin' on my dogs. Well, my Airedale anyway. Maybe that little lady will develop a little bit a-caution. She's sure gonna need it. So I climbed out of that canyon and shore enough that little ole bear is a-stickin' out there just like a sore thumb. Well I picked up a rock and flung it at that little ole bear and hit that thing square in the middle of his forehead and killed him deader than a doornail! So much for my dog trainin'....

Well, I took this little ole bear home and hung him up in my garage. Well about that time my kids and the Mexican kids got out of school, and they gathered around to see what the trapper had got. I told the 2 oldest boys to git out the skinnin' knives and jerk the hide offa that bear. This would be their chance. Now those boys were pretty handy. It wasn't too long until those boys had that hide layin' on the ground. And there was a little Spanish boy there peekin' and a-lookin'. He said, "Mr. Trapper, where did you shoot that bear?" I said, "Oh, I didn't bother to shoot a little feller like this. I just picked up a rock and I got him." Now my youngest boy was not old enough to go to school either. He was just oohing and aahing right along with the rest of the kids. He said, "Daddy, that looks just like a person hangin' there, don't it?" Well it dad-blamed shore did. Well when that young 'un said that them Mexican boys flew out of my garage in a cloud of dust just like a bunch of quail. They went in every direction.

Well, my wife and I was both flatlander kind of people. We could cook a deer or an antelope or an elk, but we didn't know how to cook a bear. And, finally I thought of old Dave Boyd, a chuckwagon cook for the Diamond A Ranch right there in the Turkey Mountains. So I went down to Dave's place. Now ole Dave was one of those old timers that had a big handlebar mustache. He probably would have weighed 135-140 pounds if he would have been dipped in salt water. But he had a 400 pound voice. I said, "Dave, do you know how to cook a bear?" He said, "Hell, yes, I can cook a bar. Can't you cook one of 'em?" I said, "Hell no. I wouldn't be down here if I knowed how to cook one." He said, "All right, so now you git you a Dutch oven. You young whipper snappers don't know much about one of them thar things. Now you git that Dutch oven about half full of grease and git it rollin' hot. And, you chunk that bear meat up jus like it was pork. It's very similar. Just accordin' to how old the bar is and what he's been a-fattened on, and you just cook the hell out of that bear meat for the better part of an hour. And, when you think it's done, you stick a fork in it now and then to try and figger it, and when you think it's done, you throw the pot and all out in the damned alley. You jus got thru a-ruinin' a damned good Dutch oven!"

Arrested?

Well I had my pickup truck in the shop there having something done to it. I had a big ole district and it was rough, and it was hard on equipment. Well, a local game warden from Los Amigos come along. I recognized him and he did me, and I walked out to the curb to meet him. And, I said, "Mike, what brings you to our neck of the woods?" He said "Darth, I've got one of the sorriest kinda jobs I've ever had to do in all of my life." And, I said, "Mike, I'll help you a whole lot. I'll help you right now."

Now, I'd made Mike a whole lot of cases. Some of them city slickers'd, you know, come out there and spotlight a big buck, cut the horns outa him and maybe take a hind quarter to brag about a little later on. Now them little nesters up there, them natives, would tell me what it was all about. They'd give me the make and the model of a car and how many people, and, many times, the license plate number. And, I'd turn all that information over to Mike and it wouldn't be long til he'd nailed somebody's hide on the barn. Well I could see them little old nesters a-killin' a deer and antelope to feed a wife and a bunch of hungry young 'uns. They didn't waste nothin'. They even cracked the bones and made soup out of 'em. Well, after all I'd rather see them kill a deer and antelope if the killer never got catched, and I let them know about it.

And, I said, "Mike, I've helped you a lot now. What'd ya got?" He reached inside of his jacket pocket and he pulled out a long piece of envelope and my name was right across the front of it. "Well," he said, "here it is." And, he handed it to me. I opened that thing up and it was a citation for taking a big game animal with an illegal weapon - a rock. I said, "Mike, what in the Devil does this here mean? What kind of a joke you got a-goin'?". He said, "Now, Darth, this ain't no joke. I never was more serious in all of my life. If there were 2 men in the State of New Mexico that I thought could interpret the Safe Game Regulations, you would be one of them men. And, you know them Regulations plainly state to take a big game animal, it will be from a firearm fired from the shoulder with a 1,000 pounds of knock down."

Well, that went all over this Indian just like wild fire. And, then I got real cool. I said, "Mike, I'll tell you what I'll do. If you'll stand out there 20 feet and let me hit you in the head with a malapai rock as big as what I hit that bear with, and if you don't swear that I've got a 1,000 pounds of knock down, then damn you, I'll plead guilty." Well, he turned just as white as one of 'um could ever git and he climbed in his pickup and he left.

Well, I ain't heard no more about that rock or that bear or that citation either. But, for the next 10 or 12 years we had a lot of that 'cat and mouse' and a whole lot of that 'touch and go'. It seems he wasn't quite through a-fightin' that battle of the Alamo.

I let my supervisor there in Albuquerque know every move that I made and why that I made it. I told him I thought he had a right to know 'cause he's helped me keep things on the right track. He said, "Darth, has he started in on you now?" I said, "I don't know, but it sure looks like it, if that's what you want to call it." He said, "I'm gonna have a talk with that boy." He called him up and he said, "Mike, if you don't get outa the hair of my hunter there in Wagon Mound, that Indian is very likely to stop up a canyon with you. I want you to listen. I want you to listen real good." Well, I think that he did. At least I hope he did. But, we've still continued to have that little bit of the 'cat and the mouse', but he didn't get any more game violation cases come out of my District, I can tell you now.

Cattlegrowers' Meetin'

My boss man called me early one spring and said, "Darth, I guess you're aware that the New Mexico Cattle Growers' is a-havin' a meetin' right here in Albuquerque, and it'll start day after tomorrow. And, I want you to arrange your affairs so you can be down here and do a little bit of public relations work for us. Now, you get along real good with the ranchers, the landowners, and the sporting people, and somebody up at our regional office at Denver has took notice of your end-of-the-year reports and some of them fellas want to meet you."

Well, when it come "going" morning there in Wagon Mound, it was snowing right straight down. Well, that wasn't nothin' new to me, and I'd probably run out of it between Santa Fe and Las Vegas. Well, that ain't the way it turned out. It snowed on me every step of the way plumb in to Albuquerque. When I got through follerin' them big trucks into there, it begin to look like I was just about the only idiot that was left out on the highway that was drivin' a pickup truck. So, I went to lookin' around for a place to stay. Now, I wouldn't a-know'd who to call anyway to make reservations. So, I'm just a-takin' my thank-you's. With that late snow storm, you know, and the meetin' of the Cattlegrowers, and most of them had made reservations, and those travelers that was stranded, it begin to look like I wasn't going to find a place. Everything I could look at had a "no vacancy" sign. Well, after a while I had one of them motel fellers a-callin' around all over town to find me a place to stay. After a while, one of them said, "We've found a place. It's a great big double room with an archway between 'em. They can put a curtain. They've done it a number of times. You will only have to share the bath." I said, "You tell that man to save that room for me. I'll be right there." He said, "Mister, I'm not tellin' that man nothin'. You better talk to him." Well, I jumped on that telephone and I said, "Oh, partner, save that room for me." And, he said, "Mister, I'm not a-savin' nothin' til you walk right up here to my desk and pay your money." I said, "Mister, will you tell me where in the devil to go a-lookin' for that place."

Well, he told me...way the hell and gone across town there somewhere, and I finally found it (with the help of a City policeman). And, I started up to his desk with my little ole suitcase. I sorta put my hand up and said, "Oh, partner, I'm the man that called about that room." And, there was a lady that walked right up by my side. She said, "Yes, and I did, too." And, this motel man said, "Now just hold on a minute. I don't want to suggest something that might be improper. Now, this is a great big double room with an archway. We've put a curtain up a number of times. You will only have to share the bath."

I said, "Lady, I'm a family man. I'm a hunter for the United States Wildlife Service, and considered a pretty decent kind of a fella. And, I would appreciate any consideration that you could give me. Nevertheless, I just hope you don't make me sleep in this here motel lobby tonight." Well, you know, that ole gal just looked me over from head to toe, just like she was a-fixin' to buy a horse.

"Well," she said, "Mister, I need a place to stay and you to do, too. Let's just sign that motel register." Well, she signed her name and I signed mine, and we paid our money. Well, I picked up the suitcases and she picked up the keys, and we hunted up that great big double room.

She was pretty nice lookin' ole gal and had all the ear marks of a country gal, and a little bit of a twinkle in her eye. I said, "Lady, pick out the place you wanna roll your bed." She kinda waved her hand and said, "Put 'er right there, cowboy. That looks good enough for me." Well, I throwed my little ole suitcase on the other bed, you know. It didn't take a whole lot for a government trapper, not back in them days, it didn't. I had a couple a-pair of socks, a comb, and a razor, and a clean shirt and a change of drawers.

Well, I went on back down to the lobby, you know, and looked around to see if I might find a lounge. Well, I had a beer, you know, and eat a bite and I bought me a magazine, and I come up to go to bed. Well, somebody had come up and put that curtain up, and the lady had already gone to bed. And, when I turned my light out, that lady said, "Mister, would you get me a glass of water, please." And, I thought, what in the hell is that ole gal a-drivin' at? Well, I'll just give her a little somethin' to think about. And, I said, "Lady, how would you like to be my wife for the rest of the night?" Well, she thought about it a little bit, I guess. She said, "Well, I guess it would be all right." And, I said "Lady, you just get your own glass of water 'cause that's exactly what my wife would have to do."

Well, when that Cattlegrowers' meetin' got over with 4 days later, and all that public relations, and I got home, there was a neighbor and his wife that was visitin' with us, Marion and Harriett Wiggins. One thing kinda led to another and I told about what happened. And, Marion Wiggins looked over at my wife and said, "What do you think about that?" She said, "I'm not too sure that old boy didn't get up and get that ole gal a glass a water!"

Lori's Buck

A couple of summers ago, Ray McGee and his lovely bride, Lori, and I went on a token lion hunt in August. We went through a low saddle and a Coues deer doe bolted out practically from under our horses. Fortunately, we were all riding gentle bulletproof horses or we might have had a wreck. Ray said, "I'll bet that doe has a fawn here close by." So we got to looking around, and Ray spotted the newborn fawn lying flat on the ground in a sotol bush. Ray got off his horse and walked like he was going to walk past the fawn. When he was close, he threw his jacket on top of the fawn and caught it. It couldn't have been over two days old. The hounds didn't even smell it (newborn fawns don't have any scent). After the hounds were well down the trail we put the fawn back exactly where it was, uninjured. The hounds were never the wiser. Lori loved the little buck. He was sure cute.

Lori McGee with newborn Coues Deer buck.

Sonora, Mexico Coues Deer Hunt

By Michael Braegelmann and Zona Pinto

Our Mexico Coues deer hunt began as a result of receiving a large pile of "pink slips" from the Arizona Game and Fish Department. My wife, Zona, and I had applied for a total of 10 permits in Arizona, plus others in New Mexico, and all were unsuccessful. Most hunters can appreciate the sense of despair and frustration we were feeling at having nothing to hunt come fall.

The day after the Arizona draw, I talked to Kirk Kelso of Pusch Ridge Outfitters to see if he had any late openings in Mexico. He was booked full, so we had all but decided that this year was a bust. Lo and behold, a couple of days later, Kirk phoned me to see if I was still looking for a hunt as he had two clients cancel on an early December hunt in Mexico for Coues. I quickly grabbed the opportunity, and the paperwork began!

The hunt preparation consisted of several outings to the Tucson Rifle Club for some much-needed practice. I had purchased a new Weatherby Accumark in .300 Weatherby Magnum and wanted to use it on the hunt. Kirk suggested that I purchase a 6.5x20 Leupold scope that had been modified with extra stadia wires to help me with my long range shooting. I gave the rifle to Kirk. He mounted the scope on it, and even worked up a very accurate handload for me. Now that's above and beyond the norm for an Outfitter! The rifle was shooting very well, and I had a crosshair for 300, 400 and 500 yards.

In early December we flew from Tucson to Hermosillo, Sonora without a hitch. Kirk met us at the airport and helped us through customs. In no time we were loaded in the Suburban and heading for the ranch. Although the ranch was very remote, the accommodations were comfortable.

Joining us on the hunt were Skip Donau and Bert Vargas from Tucson, and Fred Daum from Oregon. More about their success later!

The first morning, Zona and I were glassing with our guides, Jim Reynolds and Alex Valencia. Having hunted Coues deer in Arizona, we were not prepared for the quantity and quality of bucks we were seeing! In the first hour we had seen four bucks that were in the 100" B&C range! One huge buck gave us the slip into a forest of ocotillo cactus, and two others gave us the slip after an exciting stalk. What a morning!

After a short lunch break, we headed to higher country for more glassing. Once again, the quality and quantity of bucks were shocking! Late in the day we were busy watching three different bucks scattered across a far away hillside when Alex quietly whispered, "Muy grande," and pointed across the canyon. I wasn't so impressed with the buck, as I had been looking at him for some time through my 15x60 Zeiss binoculars. After a minute or two of my broken Spanish and his broken English, I discovered he was looking at a deer bedded in the shade on a hillside closer than the one my buck was on. After finding the buck in the binos, I agreed that this was truly a "MUY GRANDE"!

We were at least 1200 yards across the canyon from him, and losing light fast, so the quiet stalk wasn't so quiet! Jim, Alex and I moved, or should I say slid, down the hill with Zona close behind. I guess we were making more noise than we thought as the buck stood from his bed and began to work his way to the top of the ridge. When we were as close as we could get, we began frantically searching with our binoculars to try to relocate this bruiser. Jim found him standing behind an oak tree that my laser range finder was reading at 503 yards. I quickly set up for the shot and waited from him to step out.

We had less than 10 minutes of light remaining when Jim said, "He's moving uphill." I was prepared for him to move around the tree and show himself, but with the tree between us, he moved up and straight away. Finally he stepped into our view at the top of the ridge and stood quartering away from me. Jim took a laser reading on him at 551 yards. The shot was going to be at a steep uphill angle, so I laid the 500 stadia line on his shoulder and squeezed the trigger. No one saw the buck run off or go down. We had no idea what had happened until we made the hike across the canyon in the dark to see. Not five yards from where he had stood laid my buck! We were stunned with the size of his rack! He was later officially scored for Boone and Crockett at 137 0/8 gross and 128 2/8 net! This with approximately 11" of antler broken off!

The next three days were spent looking for a buck for Zona. On the fourth day, Kirk joined us to help locate the buck that had given us the slip the first day. We worked our way to the spot, set up our equipment, and, believe it or not, he was bedded under the same tree as he was on the first day! This time it was decided that our first day mistake of trying to get too close wasn't going to happen again, so Kirk, Zona and Alex set out to a vantage point that Kirk felt would present a shot, while Jim and I stayed behind with the binos.

What seemed like an eternity passed as we watched the bedded buck and waited for them to get to the predetermined spot to shoot from. We were watching the buck when he suddenly lurched forward and the report from the rifle echoed down the canyon to us. Kirk had decided that after studying the situation and knowing that Zona was shooting his rifle, that she could kill him from a different position than had been previously decided. After patiently setting up his David Miller Marksmen rifle, Zona made an incredible 494 yard one-shot kill on this magnificent 109 7/8" non-typical buck.

This type of hunting requires the best in optics and equipment. You must have quality binoculars and spotting scopes, and the ability and patience to sit behind them for hours. You must also have a rifle and ammunition capable of accurately shooting at great distances. That equipment, coupled with many trips to the range with Kirk, practicing at 300, 400 and 500 yards, resulted in our having a very successful hunt.

You can have the best of optics and equipment and be the best shooter possible, but your odds will improve dramatically with an outfitter like Kirk and guides like Jim and Alex! Every aspect of the hunt was great. The food was plentiful and delicious, and the vehicles were all 4-wheel drive, ¾ ton Suburbans in excellent condition and equipped for the rough Mexican ranch roads. The guides had all of the latest Swarovski optics and were highly skilled at finding and judging the trophy quality of each animal.

The hunt was a great success, by any measure, for all of us in camp. Skip Donau took a tremendous 114 1/8" B&C buck, Fred Daum took a great 109 4/8" buck, and Bert Vargas took a very respectable 100" deer!

Zona Pinto and
Michael Braegelmann
with Mexican Coues deer.

The Successful Lion Hunt

By Allen O. Brandt

(Written at age ten)

One Sunday morning in September of '94, my Dad and I decided to go lion hunting in the Santa Rita Mountain Range right behind our house. So that morning my Dad and I loaded the dogs and the horses. Just then, I looked up in the sky and saw a falling star. That was when I knew we were going to catch my trophy Tom mountain lion.

When we drove up to our camp site we parked, unloaded the dogs and saddled the horses. We were riding for quite a while. After we went over a peak called Castle Dome, the dogs hit a track. We waited a while to see what they were trailing. We lost the dogs after a few minutes and got my Dad's tracking device. We went to where we thought we got the best signal and we found the dogs right where we thought they would be. The dogs had a pretty fresh track. My dad and I went to the water hole by where the dogs were trailing. Sure enough, a fresh lion track, but it looked like the dogs were going the wrong way. We tried to turn the dogs around but they didn't want to go that way. So we let the dogs go the way they wanted to go, about two minutes later they jumped a big Tom lion.

We got off our horses and went to the tree. The dogs we had were Ike, Drifter, and Buck. My Dad laid me down so I had a steady shot, but it really was one of the most uncomfortable positions. I shot once but the scope was foggy! I shot twice but the rock was digging into my hip! I shot three times and, boom, I got him!

After we field dressed out the lion and everything, I asked my Dad, "Where's the camera for my picture with the lion?" He said, "I forgot it." I said, "What?" He said, "We will take a picture at the truck." We were about to put the lion on my saddle to pack it out, but when we tried to lift him it was impossible. So my Dad said, "We will come back to pick him up with the truck."

As we were going back to the truck, the dogs hit a red hot track. I thought to myself, could they catch another lion? My Dad said, "Look on the side of that hill!" Sure enough, I saw him. It was a big black bear. My Dad called and called the dogs to let the bear go, but they wouldn't listen; they were too busy chasing a bear! After he called the dogs back to the horses he could hardly talk.

When we got back to the truck, we left to go find my lion. By the time we got there, I was worn out thinking we were never going to find my lion again. We finally found him and loaded him on the truck, and my Dad took a picture of me and my lion. Then we went home. When we got home I told my Mom we had a successful hunt and got back with all the dogs......we even got a record book Mountain Lion. The skull measured 14.2 after the 60 day dry period.

This year I hope I do just as good at shooting a lion as I did last year.

Author's note: This was a rare case where the lion was killed near a ranch road. Under most circumstances, we would have skinned the lion on the spot. Allen wanted to bring his out in one piece.

Allen Brandt, age 10, with trophy male lion.

1994

Allen Brandt roping a calf with "River" at the Arizona Junior Rodeo in Willcox, AZ at age 10, where he won a buckle for 1st place.

Muy Grande!

By Roy Haskell

I have been on 1,980 hunts so far, and have hunted extensively around the world. I have always wanted to shoot a big record book mule deer.

In 1993 I booked a hunt with "Campillo Brothers Sonoran Trophy Hunts" in Sonora, Mexico. I was scheduled to hunt in November of '93.

They picked me up in a Ford Bronco at the Hermosillo Airport, in Mexico. I had my faithful .30-06 Remington model 700 with me. They took care of the gun permit and all the paperwork.

The trip to the Ranch was uneventful. The cold beer was "delicioso."

The "Rancho Dotil' where we camped and hunted was west of Hermosillo, about 20 miles from Baja, California. The ranch house was very comfortable with 20,000 acres of surrounding mule deer habitat.

The 1st day there it rained all nite (over 1" total). We were anxious to go hunting.

The guides in Mexico hunt a little differently than we do in Arizona. They track the deer as opposed to glassing them up with binoculars, like I am used to.

After a good breakfast, four guides and myself starting driving the ranch roads looking for tracks. After about 30 minutes, we saw where a deer had crossed the road. A closer inspection revealed it was a big buck track. The guides went 1st and I followed close behind. (This country is thick Mesquite and Palo Verde. It is hard to see for over 100 yards.) After tracking this deer for about 45 minutes, the lead guide stopped in his tracks. He motioned over to his right. The guide closest to me saw the buck and pointed him out to me. This buck was about 80 yards away, standing still. I asked the guide if I should shoot. (They were all aware of the fact that I was looking for a big deer.) "Muy grande!" whispered the guide. I centered the crosshairs of my gun and touched off a round. The buck ran a short distance and fell dead. A perfect heart shot.

The guides and I were excited. This was an extra nice buck. He field dressed at 258 lbs. and scored 209 7/8 points with a 35" spread. In 1993 this buck scored number 3 in the S.C.I Trophy Book.

The next 9 days I enjoyed the good life in camp: eating "Carne Asada," made from my deer and drinking booze.

Three other hunters shot a mule deer while I was there; none were as big as mine.

The Mexican guides spoke a little English and I spoke a little Spanish. The food and drink was great, as was their warm hospitality.

After almost 2,000 hunts (not all for mule deer!) I finally got my "Muy Grande Venado."

"Muy Grande"
Roy Haskell, Sonora, Mexico 1993

The One of a Kind Trophy

By Shane Lyman

At the end of December 2000, I got a call from a local rancher that said he had a steer that had been killed by a lion. Earlier in the year, I was riding for this ranch and noticed a couple other old kills and thought there may have been a lion killing the steers, but thought it somewhat unlikely because the ranch was in low grass lands and the steers were healthy 400-600 lbs. If it was a lion, I thought it had to be a large tom.

I went in the evening to take a look at the kill. It was a lion kill still covered, but it smelled pretty bad so I was not very optimistic about the lion returning that night. Later I called Buck to see if he wanted to go with me in the morning, and he did. We met the rancher just before daybreak and rode to the kill. As soon as the dogs got near the kill the whole pack blew up, pups and all, running and bawling on the track at a full run. They trailed for about 3/4 of a mile and treed the lion in a large cottonwood; to my surprise it was an averaged sized female. I shot the lion out of the tree and we began to take some pictures. As I looked down to hold the lion's head up, I noticed a silver piece of aluminum sticking out of the lion's forehead. At closer examination I found it to be an aluminum arrow shaft sticking out of its forehead about a half inch and the lion's left eye was blind, explaining why she was taking large livestock and eating rotting meat. I cleaned the skull up and also discovered a three bladed broad head imbedded in the left eye socket. The bone had grown completely around and through the grooves of the broad head. Apparently, an archery hunter had hit the lion and not been able to recover it. It looked as though the lion had had the piece of arrow in its head for a least a year or two. I have been offered quite a bit of money for the skull, but plan to hold onto it. It will probably be a while before I find another one like it.

One of a kind trophy.

Caught by Shane Lyman and Buck Garner.

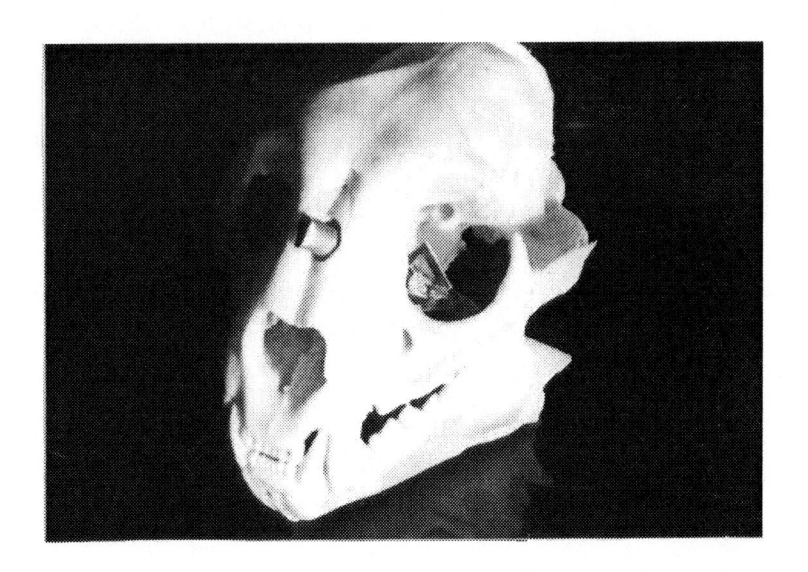

Treed!

Ken Lange and Buck Garner

Colorado Elk

A number of years ago, my dad, Fritz Selby, Curt Beyers, and I made a trip to Colorado to hunt elk. Curt was from that country and knew the area well.

We left in the afternoon and drove all night. I trailered two horses and stopped a couple of times to walk the horses around. The next morning we stopped in Grand Junction to charter a plane and do some scouting. The area we were to hunt was in the Book Cliff Mountains in Southwest Colorado. We saw quite a few elk from the air. There were a few good bulls.

We made camp and the first morning dad and I went one way, and Curt and Fritz another. Dad and I rode horseback until we got into elk country. Then we tied up the horses. Dad's back was bothering him a little, so I had him watch a saddle that I thought I could move some elk through. I made a big circle on foot. I had located some elk with my binoculars, and I wanted to push them to Dad. All of the cows went through the saddle. There were two bulls, a lessor bull and a nice six-point. The bulls split from the herd, and when I found them again they were moving up the mountain. They were a long ways off, I guessed about 700 yards. I knew I had but one chance. I started shooting, but I couldn't tell where I was hitting. I kept shooting higher and higher, hoping luck would prevail, as it does so often for me. After the 7th shot I couldn't find the big bull. I kept looking and looking and I finally found him sliding down the mountain. When Dad heard the shooting stop he walked down to where I was. "What in the world are you doing, son?" "I just shot an elk, Dad," I said, "and it is on the side of that mountain over there." Dad looked where I was pointing and exclaimed, "You didn't kill an elk that far away!" I assured him I did and we took off walking. I decided to have some fun with Dad. On the way to where this elk was I said, "I hope this bull has 4 points. I think it does." (We were hunting in a four-point or better area). Now I had Dad concerned. He moaned, "Holy cow, here we are a thousand miles from home, hunting as a non-resident in Colorado, and you shoot at an elk you are not sure of the size!" I let him worry all the way to the elk. When we got close to where this bull was, I told Dad I wasn't exactly sure where he was. "You look over in this area and check around over here." I pointed Dad to the location of this bull. I waited and waited. After a while Dad yelled, "I found your elk. You were bull shitting me again!" He was a dandy six-point bull. The 7th shot had broken his back. We field dressed him and went back for the horses.

The next morning Fritz and Curt were good enough to help us pack out the meat, head, and horns. My horse was not too fond of the elk antlers poking him in the ass. He had packed out quite a few lions, but no elk. He finally settled down and we made for camp.

Fritz and Curt were a big help on this hunt. I count them both among my friends. Elk hunting is a lot of fun until an elk is killed. Then it stops being fun and starts being real hard work.

Author with six-point
Bull elk (Colorado) and Sorley

Tried and True

By Shane Lyman

In mid-January of 2001, about two days after a rain, my brother, Wade, and I saddled up the mules and headed out to make a circle in the Canelo Hills just south of my home. Two different individuals told me of a large lion track they had seen. After unloading Bell, a trained lion dog, and Sam, one of Layne's pups, and my two pups (Chip and Blue), we started down a two-track road and hit a trail close to where the lion tracks had been seen. The air was damp and cool and the dew dripped off of the vegetation. (This is very unusual in our part of the country.)

Just after we crossed a small arroyo, Bell opened up like she had hit a fresh lion track. She trailed out of the canyon and up and over another ridge with the pups close behind. They were bawling and trailing for all they were worth. We spurred the mules and got to the top of a small ridge to listen for the dogs. To my amazement, the dogs were a good mile away trailing up a ridge into prime lion country. As we rode to catch up, Blue came back to us near the top of a large crest, and the other two dogs were not to be found. This was unlike Blue who normally could not be pried from the old dogs. We finally topped out on the big ridge, got off of our mules and strained to listen for Bell's steady chop. She was down at the edge of a stock pond. As we continued riding down the steep rocky ridge, the closer we got to Bell, the more things just didn't seem right. The steady chops were not as continuous and she seemed to hesitate a little. That wasn't like Bell. When she has a lion treed, she tells the whole world and hardly stops to breathe. We got to within 100 yards and I finally saw what all of the ruckus was about. My jaw hit the ground. I couldn't believe my eyes. Bell was on the shore of the stock pond and had one of the biggest Coues whitetail bucks I had ever seen standing in the middle of the pond. I yelled at Bell and she stopped barking for a short time, but went back to barking. I had to physically go grab her from the edge of the pond. As I grabbed Bell, the deer swam to the opposite edge of the pond and just laid at the water's edge.

I took a few pictures of the deer to make sure Layne would believe me. I estimated the deer to score about 125 inches Boone and Crockett. Bell trailed that deer for approximately 5-7 miles and just plumb wore him out. I called Layne to tell him what had happened thinking he would be mad, but when he heard the story he just laughed and couldn't hardly believe it. Bell had probably crossed a thousand deer tracks before that time, and had deer jump right in front of her, without so much as even lifting her head. The only thing we can figure is the buck was in the middle of the rut and left more scent on this particularly damp morning.

After that wreck, she went back to being the tried and true lion dog that she was; a great hound in every respect.

Shane Lyman with Bell

Dr. Green's Virgin Elk Hunt

By Gilbert Smith

Many years ago when I was still guiding for elk, I agreed to take Dr. Green, a physician from Illinois, on a Wyoming elk hunt in the northwest corner of Wyoming between Jackson Hole and Dubois. I had hunted and guided extensively in this area for many years.

I was born and raised on a homestead ranch near Laramie, Wyoming. I have raised cattle and sheep and operated equipment, but hunting was always my hobby and a way to supplement my income. I have guided hunters on hundreds of elk, deer, and antelope hunts. Coyote hunting with snowmobiles is a great pastime of mine.

I met Doc Green and his wife in Dubois, and we prepared for the hunt. The first thing we did was check to see that his rifle was sighted in. It appeared to be shooting fine. We proceeded to camp where everyone was introduced to one another. My wife, Shirley (a wonderful camp cook), had made some pies for dessert. We all enjoyed a fresh piece of homemade pie and hot coffee.

Doc Green had a speech impediment. He stuttered sometimes when he was talking. It was amusing, and it didn't bother Doc Green at all.

The first morning, when we got up, it was snowing real hard. We decided to wait out the storm and sit around camp and tell huntin' stories and cut firewood. Doc Green was real impatient and wanted to get out and go huntin'. The storm let up some around 11:00 a.m. I laid some topo maps on the table to show Doc Green where Devil's Basin was, and where I was going to take him on his virgin elk hunt. Devil's Basin is a canyon about three miles across and ten miles long, and it takes about a day to walk from one end to the other. I showed him on the map some of the tributaries and trails of the area. Doc Green always packed a compass. I asked him if I could see his compass. He laid it on the table. I asked him if he could tell me where North is. He studied this compass for awhile and said, "I think North must be where the needle is pointing, but it doesn't seem like North to me." I assured him that the compass was right. I told him if, at any time, he became confused about where he was to go East and climb up the mountain. When you get on top there will be jeep tracks and trails and you can follow those tracks back to the camp.

I told Doc Green that we would hunt towards Devil's Basin. I told him we might get separated in the thick timber. "If we do, don't cross any creeks that you can't dip dry with a 5-gallon bucket." Doc and I hunted down country until we could see the creek in Devil's Basin. I told Doc, "Whatever you do, do not cross that creek or you will get lost, and we will have a problem." I have done lots of guiding and I know how confusing strange country can be to folks that aren't familiar with these mountains. I told Doc to hunt up the creek until he came to a horse trail, and then take the horse trail back to camp. I told him I would walk around the mountain and try to drive some elk his way. I told him to walk slow, and there are several "parks" (meadows), and to look the parks over real good. These elk like to feed in these parks. "If you don't see any elk by 2:00 p.m., start heading for camp." I left Doc there, crossed the canyon and walked around the mountain. I spooked a few elk, but they went north to an area where Doc would not have been able to see them. On my way back to camp, I cut the tracks of a hunter. I was concerned they were Doc's tracks, and, if they were, he was going the wrong way! I couldn't tell for sure if they were Doc's tracks because it was snowing and I couldn't make out exactly what the tread mark looked like. I felt sure it was Doc's tracks, so I decided to follow them. After a little ways, these tracks went into a large park. It was snowing so hard by then that the tracks were completely covered up and I couldn't follow them any further.

I sure hoped at that point that Doc was going to be able to find his way back to camp. I started back to camp myself, and on the way I saw fresh bear tracks. The tracks were headed towards camp, so I decided to follow them for a ways. I could see that this bear went into a thicket where there was a spring with water that never freezes. There were some white berries of some kind that this bear was feeding on. I decided to try some myself. They tasted pretty good. I don't know what those berries were, but I guess I ate too many. When I decided I had enough, I could hardly walk. It was like I was drunk! I decided to quit following the bear tracks at that point and head for camp. I had a little explaining to do when I got to camp, 'cause I was acting a little goofy. The worse news was Doc wasn't in camp. It was starting to get dark. I hurried over to a little point where I could see out over the canyon and fired a shot. Sure enough, Doc fired back with two shots. He was clear across the canyon, exactly where I told him not to go! I took a couple of flashlights and drove the Jeep as far as I could in the direction where I thought I heard Doc shoot. I fired another shot and Doc answered again. He was two or three miles away, going the wrong way! I was concerned I would never be able to catch up with him in the dark. I decided to spend the night in camp and leave early in the morning to find him. I was quite sure he could last one night out. My wife, Shirley, was not very happy with me. I was sure hoping he would wind up in another hunting camp.

The next morning was clear and good weather - a good day to look for a lost hunter. Hopefully, we would find Doc alive. Another hunter and I took chainsaws and a Jeep and followed a horse trail into the area that Doc was in. Before long we found the tracks of a hunter going in both directions. At that point we weren't sure what was going on. We kept following the horse trail and blazing the road until we came out on a Jeep trail that came in from the other direction. We started down that Jeep trail when suddenly we heard a shot not far from where we were. Up above us was Doc, waving his arms. We went up there, and Doc was so excited and stuttering so bad he could hardly talk. He finally told us that he ran into another camp and these hunters told him he needed to be on the other side of the Basin. They told Doc he could spend the night with them. Doc declined and said he would make it to camp okay. On his way back to camp his flashlight gave out. He almost poked his eyes out when he got into the thick timber. Then he realized he couldn't even find his way back to the other hunters' camp! He was stuck. Doc tried unsuccessfully to start a fire with wet wood. He had a plastic type survival blanket with him, so he wrapped himself up in that. He said he might have slept for thirty minutes or so. He was so miserable he couldn't sleep. Come daylight he made his way back to the other hunters' camp. He knew where it was! We picked Doc up and headed for our camp. Doc explained, "I...I...I...I...I shot a nice three point mule deer buck yesterday." Doc wasn't sure if he could find the deer again. I told him we would look for it. I had an idea where it might be. When we got into the timber a ways, I stopped to look for tracks. In the timber, the snow doesn't cover up the tracks as quick as it does in those open parks. I found Doc's tracks and back-tracked until his tracks went into a patch of quakey Aspens. (Doc told me he shot that buck in some quakeys.) We drove the Jeep as close as we could. After awhile we located Doc's mule deer and dragged it to the Jeep. Doc waited in the Jeep for us. He was give out.

We started back to camp with Doc's buck in the back of the Jeep. We stopped at the bottom of a steep hill to tighten the tire chains on the Jeep. Doc said, "Gil, I've read a lot of hunting stories. Most guides will not take hunters into real rough country, where the game is, until after they have hunted for a few days. Is that your game plan?" I said, "Doc, you have done a lot of reading, but not much hunting. What you are getting here is some practical experience. We have been in elk habitat since we got here!" It was a steep climb out of that canyon. We kicked up a lot of rocks, dirt and snow getting back on top. When we finally got to camp, we hung Doc's buck on a meat pole. We had a good area to hang up game in the shade where the sun never did shine.

It was a cold day and snowing, so we all went into the tent to warm up. I had built a special stove for this tent, with the pipe going underground and sticking up about 10 ft. on the outside of the tent. Doc went in and sat down on this hot stove, for about two seconds! He jumped up and yelled, "that, that, that box is hot!" "Yeah, Doc" I said. "You just sat on the stove." If he hadn't been wearing some real thick pants, he could have been seriously burned. Doc couldn't believe that I had built a stove without a stovepipe inside the tent. He had to go outside and see for himself!

There were a few elk killed during the next four days, but not very many. Doc never got a shot. After the snow, most of the elk had moved to lower country. Doc was a little discouraged, but not too bad.

The fifth day of the hunt, I decided to take Doc to town. I told him to keep his rifle handy, and be ready to load a shell into the chamber if we saw an elk. On the way to town I saw several elk coming off the mountain, headed our way. I told Doc, "There's a five-point bull elk in the herd. Get out and get ready to shoot!" Doc jumped out of the truck and pumped a round into his Remmington pump action .30-60 rifle, and shot into the ground 20 ft. in front of the pickup! Doc pumped another round into his rifle, and about that time that bull elk stopped to see what in the world was going on. Doc shot and killed that bull elk not 30 ft. from the road. He was elated! It didn't take us long to field dress that bull and wrestle him into the back of the truck. We proceeded to town to the meat locker so they could butcher Doc's elk and deer. Doc decided to stay an extra day so the meat packing in Dubois could cut and wrap his animals. He and his wife would spend the day looking around Jackson and would pick up the meat the following day, ice the meat down, and drive back to Illinois.

Doc has hunted with me many times after that. He and I became friends, he learned how to use a compass, how to find his way around, and became a pretty good hunter.

Author's note: Gil Smith has been a friend of the Brandt family for a long time. He and his family are good friends and good people and good hunters.

Gil Smith, Laramie, Wyoming

(Photo taken in Author's trophy room in Continental, Arizona. 2001)

Rena's Lion

By Ollie Barney

This is the story of a hunt I started several years ago. Every year I donate a 3-day hunt to the Safari Club to auction off at the annual fund-raiser. I had wanted Rena Rios to buy this hunt so I talked to Chuck (Rena's husband) and told him that if any of the local members bought the hunt I would add a couple of days to it to give them a better chance of getting a lion. I was sure he would buy the hunt for Rena or I wouldn't have offered the extra two days.

As it turned out, Rena bought the hunt herself and paid a good price for it. When it came time to take her out though, I was a little bit apprehensive because this girl is a real lady and I wondered if she would be able to make a lion hunt in the rough and sometimes bad country we have to go through. But Chuck told me not to worry, that she was tough, and I found out that she is tough, both physically and mentally. If all my clients were like her, I would probably still be a professional hunting guide. With people like her, it is a pleasure to hunt with them.

We went out to my old ranch and hunted for five days out there, trailed several lions, and finally caught a fox. That was a disappointment to me because I wasn't sure what the dogs had treed, but when we saw it was a fox, Rena never complained. A lot of clients would have given me a hard time over my lion dogs catching a fox and would have been more disappointed in the dogs and me both. Anyway, we made the hunt and had a good hunt, but it was unsuccessful. But I told her, "Don't give up! I'll take you out again. Some rancher will report a kill or something will come up and I'll call you." She said that was fine because "I really want a lion!" and she was deserving of a really good lion.

We went along for several months and then Layne Brandt, a friend of mine who has some hounds of his own and borrows one or two of mine sometimes, wanted to take off one Saturday and go up in the Santa Rita Mountains. There are quite a few lion in there and I knew there was a very good possibility that we might catch one. So I called Rena up and told her Layne and I were going up there the next day and if she wanted to come along to meet me at the Green Valley Post Office at 6:30 Saturday morning, and we would go on over to Layne's at Continental and leave out from there. Well, I got there at 6:00 o'clock and she was already waiting for me, ready to go.

It had snowed some the night before and we went up in Box Canyon near the top, parked up there and turned the dogs loose. We started across country and hunted probably for two hours. The dogs hit a track and went off into West Sawmill Canyon clear down to the bottom of it. We couldn't get down there so we came back down the trail for about a mile-and-a-half and rode out where we might hear the dogs in the canyon, but we couldn't hear anything. Back to the south of us, the wind had come up and we could hear the dogs barking. They just seemed to stay in the same place, so I told Layne and Rena, "Hell, those dogs are not moving." So we followed the trail back for about three-quarters of a mile and climbed up into a saddle. About a quarter of a mile from us, there was my dog, Blackie, plus Sport and Abe, with a lion treed. There was no way we could get in there horseback, it was so rough. We tied our horses up, Rena got her gun, and we started off down in there. It was pretty treacherous going. There weren't any bluffs to fall off of, but you could slide ten feet and get yourself badly skinned up if you weren't careful.

I cut me off a Sotol pole to use for a Moses stick to help me along, then got one for Rena, but Layne was making it on his own, and I'm in the lead. We get down in there and the tree the lion was in was a big old half-dead juniper. The lion was on the far side of the juniper and we couldn't see him from the uphill side, so we circled around where we could see into the side of the tree, about 30 yards away. I could see the lion's head and I showed it to Rena. She had to shoot off hand, so I got my Moses stick out there so she could rest her rifle on that and I'm holding it steady. About that time the old lion kind of raised his head up a little bit and exposed his neck, and she shot immediately. She is a good shot and I heard the lion hit the ground hard and down the hill the dogs went. The snow was slick and when the dogs hit the lion they all started sliding down the mountain, with the dogs tugging on it and all going right on down together. Rena said, "It's getting away!" I said, "No, it isn't getting away because it is dead. I could tell by the way it hit the ground. It's just sliding in the snow and the dogs are dragging it." Finally, it lodged against some brush and when we got down there, it was a huge Tom, a really big one, and I would love to have weighed it. I know it weighed over 140 pounds.

Layne and I had to skin it out, since there was no way of packing it out and no way to get a horse in there. We were going to hang it up but the snow was melting and the ground underneath was frozen, so we couldn't stand up enough to hang this lion up where we wanted to. We slid it off into the bottom of a little draw where there was a stump and we got the lion behind the stump and skinned it out there. It took us about 45 minutes to an hour to skin it. Layne packed the hide out and I started packing Rena's rifle out. Jeez, she just walked off and left us! Layne and I were rimming around, Layne was packing the lion hide and it's tough going for him, and I was having a lot of trouble with my legs, which was tough on me. We got about half way out when Rena came back and took the gun. We climbed on out to our horses, but I still had some dogs down in this Sawmill Canyon. We could hear them after we'd shot the lion and then Blackie just pulled out and went down to where they were. Layne took the lion hide and went back to the truck while Rena and I were going down into Sawmill Canyon to gather up the dogs. There is a road that comes up and goes out the main road where Layne would come along and pick us up.

We got down there but the dogs were on another lion track and were trailing it. We rounded them up though, pulling them off of it, and by the time we got out to the road, it was starting to get dark. Rena's feet were getting awfully cold, as her boots had gotten wet in the snow, and she got off and walked but she never whimpered about it. I've had some men hunters who have hunted all over the world and call themselves "international hunters." If their feet would have been freezing they would have wanted to stop and build a fire or maybe get a helicopter in to take them out, but not this little old gal! She just toughed it right on out. We met Layne and loaded up our horses and the dogs and came on in.

This was one of my more enjoyable hunts and this big lion couldn't have gone to a better person than Rena.

Rena with her 2nd lion. 2000

Record Book Sheep Horns

In 1972 Dad and I decided to go hiking around in Southwest Arizona, just to have a look around. We weren't looking for sheep horns, or anything in particular. It was a nice winter day, and Dad and I always liked to see what was over the next ridge. I left the main trail and started looking into some caves. I could see where there was sign of smoke in one cave, evidence of earlier humans. I always like to look for Indian artifacts when I'm hunting or hiking. Mom's favorite hobby was looking for arrowheads. After climbing around for a while, I spotted a cave high on the mountain that looked like a likely spot for Indians to oversee their domain. After an exhausting climb, I was at the cave entrance. I couldn't believe my eyes! There was a perfect matched set of big Desert Sheep horns. They had been there so long that the skull was completely gone. It was a real chore packing those horns out. I felt sorry for the sheep that had to pack them all the time! The horns measured 187.2 inches and were #1 in the state in 1972.

State's biggest

**Record Book Desert Sheep Horns
found in remote mountain cave.**

Display of Desert Sheep horns taken at the Sheep Society meeting.

Princess, the Bucking Mule

By Jeff Dobbins

You could tell it was going to be a hot day even though it was barely 50 degrees in the hour before dawn as I waited for Layne Brandt at the Green Valley Post Office. The month of May is like that in the Sonora Desert with daytime temperatures approaching 90 degrees in the afternoon. This would probably be Layne's last lion hunt until September as it would be too hot during the summer months for mules and dogs, not to mention hunters.

It was Sunday morning and Layne had called on Thursday to invite me on a lion hunt. I had finally called Layne and asked to be put on his "Call List" after another hunter I had referred to him had captured his lion in one morning with Layne's partner, Shane Lyman. In fact, his partner had called an hour after Layne with an invitation to hunt the following morning, but I declined because of family and business obligations.

As we drove the short distance to the Tumacacori Mountains, Layne and I spoke of many things, having been introduced many years before at a Safari Club meeting. Along the way Layne stated he could not guarantee success but said he was taking me to a spot that usually produced a lion. As the stars began to disappear in the eastern sky we pulled into the bottom of an arroyo, and it was here I was introduced to "Princess", the mule. We were quickly good friends, or so I thought. Layne also introduced me to "Slik", the horse that was there to carry out the lion, and his dogs Bell, Major, Blackie, Liza and Radar. He was quick to note that he and Ollie Barney were partners on Blackie and Liza. (Major and Bell and Radar are owned by Brian Thomas.)

We were ready to begin the hunt when Layne noticed that Slik was missing a shoe on one of his hind legs. The country we would be hunting could be extremely rocky so, to protect Slik, Layne stated we would follow the road towards a spring and see what transpired. We no sooner left the truck than the hounds signaled they had scented a lion and, sure enough, we found lion tracks on the dirt road. I was thinking how easy lion hunting could be and was wondering to myself why I had never done this before. It seemed to me to be the perfect morning as I rode Princess up the road with our backs to the sun now peeking over the horizon, my pleasant conversation with Layne, and the sound of dogs barking in the distance.

The dogs started trailing slower and slower. Layne figured they were going the wrong way, so he turned the dogs around. It wasn't long until they trailed out of hearing distance. (We could see fresh lion tracks going both directions.)

All of the dogs wore radio collars and after several minutes of not being able to locate the dogs, Layne assembled his locater and pinpointed the dogs' location. It was clear the dogs were not moving so we slowly worked our way in their direction keeping in mind Slik was missing a shoe. We had crossed a small canyon and were working up towards the dogs when they suddenly moved from the peak above us through a saddle to another peak a 1/4 of a mile away. The ground was now steep and very rocky and Layne decided Slik should not go any further. I frankly was glad to get off Princess and let Layne ride her as we proceeded into the saddle.

The sound of the hounds was now clear and it appeared they had a lion cornered on the second peak. Fifty-foot cliffs made up the other side of the peak, which then tapered to the valley floor. As we approached the top, Layne handed me the scoped lever action .44 magnum he carried and quickly instructed me to pull the hammer back once I saw the lion and shoot. He forgot to tell me about the trigger safety.

We had worked our way over to the peak and were looking down the cliff side when below me about thirty-five yards I saw the mountain lion. I quickly shouldered the rifle, pulled the hammer back, and squeezed the trigger. The hammer fell but nothing happened. The trigger safety was engaged and before I figured that out the lion was gone from view. We stayed on the peak hoping to catch sight of the lion when suddenly there it was, below us maybe two hundred yards in the saddle. As it moved through chest high brush Layne said, "Shoot." My first shot was above the lion, the second was behind and by now I was getting excited! Unbelievably the lion kept walking and as I squeezed the third shot I saw it do a back flip and run towards the first peak.

The dogs were in hot pursuit as Layne and I worked our way back to Princess in the saddle. Layne suggested I walk down and thru the saddle to look for blood while he rode Princess around the ridge, as we had not seen where the lion had gone. I did not find any blood in the saddle but as I approached Layne's position he appeared and motioned me to hurry as the dogs were "barking treed".

Among the din of barking dogs you could clearly hear the hissing and growling of the lion as we approached. The lion had apparently positioned itself in a cave with the entrance now blocked by Layne's dogs. With the dogs blocking the entrance, the lion was not going anywhere but it would also be impossible to get a shot at the lion without fear of hitting one of the dogs. Layne and I sized up the situation and decided he would climb twenty feet above the dogs hoping to find a way at the lion. On the way up he turned and told me to stay where I was and if the lion came out running not to shoot. He was halfway up the cliff when I decided to start after him knowing the dogs would keep the lion from leaving and convinced we would see the lion from above. I was almost to Layne when I saw him turn wide eyed and announce the lion was on the other side of a rock he was pointing at. We both slowed down at that point because quarters were pretty cramped on the cliff and I had a loaded gun in my hand. I took his place and peeked over the rock and there, twelve inches from my face, was the back and shoulders of the lion. Layne mentioned something about not hitting the dogs when I shot and if I could see the lion. I told him I could see the lion as I lifted the gun above my head and placed the muzzle directly between the lions shoulders. At the shot the lion came rolling out of the cave and was immediately descended upon by the dogs.

Layne said not to shoot, but it was obvious the lion was not dead. The bullet had not gone through the lion's chest but instead had exited underneath the cat's right front leg because of the angle at which I had held the rifle. After a moment he asked for my knife and, as I watched wide-eyed, Layne buried his hand into the lion's chest and with that the lion expired.

We now had a chance to examine the lion, and it turned out to be a mature female, approximately 5 to 7 years old, according to Layne. We also found where my third shot had hit the lion above the spine 8 inches in front of the tail. Layne said now that his guide duties were over I had to carry the lion up the hill and then down again to Slik. I mentioned to him it would be easier to go straight down as I thought we were 300 yards above Slik. After a few moments of looking we did find a slot through the cliffs and down I went with the dogs, alternately carrying and dragging the mountain lion to the bottom while Layne rode Princess down to meet us. The dogs and I beat Layne to the bottom by a few minutes and rested in the shade of a huge boulder.

Once Layne arrived, it took only a few minutes for him to gather up the lion and load it on Slik. We were ready to leave but by that time the temperature was approaching 80 degrees, and I was completely heated up after carrying the lion. I am sure I smelled like one big pussycat. Layne said he would lead with the lion and for me to ride Princess. Layne had mentioned earlier that Princess would not carry a lion, but that was the last thing that was on my mind as I put my left foot in the stirrup.

Murphy's law says that if anything can go wrong, it will. Well, as I swung into the saddle I could tell Princess had changed her mind about us being friends. All at once she began bucking and my only thought was to get off and in a hurry. With my right foot free I thought the only course of action was to free my left foot and slide off Princess' right side. I had my left knee over the saddle when Princess decided one more buck would rid her of the lion on her back, and into the air I went horizontally.

Years before I had been trained by the Forest Service as a smokejumper on how to land in rocky conditions without getting hurt. But with my feet level with my head and five feet off the ground there was nothing to do but land like a sack of potatoes. The pain was stunning as I lay on the ground but I realized I had not heard anything crack, so given a few moments I knew I could walk. What had broken my fall was a fanny pack with my knife, empty water bottle and camera. Layne came rushing over saying Princess had never done anything like that before and offered me three Tylenol. To this day I wonder why Layne was carrying the Tylenol. Of course, Princess was standing 30 feet away looking like my best friend - now that I was off her back.

It took several minutes for us to gather up all the gear Princess had removed from her back but we were soon walking down the mountain, me leading Princess. I occasionally looked over my shoulder at her and noticed her ears were always forward and her eyes seemed larger than usual. When we reached the bottom Layne suggested he ride Princess and that I lead Slik and I thought, well you go right ahead but tell me where the Tylenol is. Layne obviously did not smell or act like a lion as he rode Princess back to the truck without incident.

From start to finish the hunt had taken a little over 4 hours and I had my lion. On the way out Layne commented he knew hunters who had spent weeks hunting for lion without success. I truly felt lucky that day, from start to finish. Several weeks later I finished the roll of film I had started on the lion hunt. To be honest I wasn't surprised when I noticed the roll of film had a big dent in it. The photos turned out just fine.

Princess

(John Bessett's mule)

Jeff Dobbins

with female lion and Radar.

Spilsbury's Hounds

David Spilsbury lived in Colonial Juarez, Chi., Mexico. He farmed and ranched there and did quite a bit of lion hunting. Two of his sons, Max and David, Jr., have both worked for "F.I.C.O." and are both good friends of mine. David, Sr. has gone to the happy hunting grounds. He and I always enjoyed visiting about hunting. I wanted to include a few of his stories in my book.

Dave used to hunt a lot with another lion hunter from El Paso, Texas (whose name I can't recall). Whenever their dogs would chase a deer, Dave would whip his friend's dogs and his friend would whip his dogs. They would never whip their own dogs.

On one hunt they found where a lion had killed a deer. All of the dogs tried to trail it up, except one, old Sam. Old Sam decided to have lunch. He ate a big bite of meat off this deer. After he ate, he took a shit and laid down in the shade and took a nap. All of the other dogs were trailing the lion. Dave's friend said, "You ought to kill old Sam. He is absolutely worthless." Dave agreed he probably should. After Sam had his siesta he got up, walked around the deer, smelled around, and starting trailing in the opposite direction from the other dogs. He only trailed a little ways until he started barking treed. He had a big tom lion caught! All the other dogs went the wrong way. Dave's friend promptly apologized for suggesting Sam needed to be killed!

One day Dave got a call from a rancher in New Mexico. This rancher had a lion killing calves. Dave said, "I will be there first thing tomorrow morning with three good dogs. You catch up a good horse for me to ride." Dave left home real early. He was at the border by daybreak. When the U.S. Customs saw him, they asked him for the rabies certificates for the dogs. Dave replied, "I don't have them with me; they are all at home."

"Then you can't bring those hounds into the U.S. until you get the papers." Dave turned around and started back when he got an idea. In this small Mexican town on the border, he found a young Mexican boy and asked him if he would like to earn $5.00. That was a lot of money in those days. The boy gladly agreed.

Dave put three short ropes on the hounds. "You hold these dogs for me. When you hear me holler, drop the ropes and let those hounds go." Dave drove back to the border (1/4 of a mile or so) and told the customs officials he was going to leave the dogs in Mexico. He was permitted to cross. A hundred yards or so down the road he stopped and yelled for his dogs. They, of course, came at a run. The dogs jumped in the truck and Dave sped off. He went to the ranch, caught the lion, and went back home. The Customs Officials really raised hell with him about what he had done, but they didn't arrest him.

One day Dave was in Deming, New Mexico picking up some supplies. A man came up to Dave and said, "I have two lion dogs that I want to give away. I have quit lion hunting, and I want them to have a good home." Dave, pleased with his good fortune, took his new hounds to his ranch in Mexico. After a week or so he decided to take those dogs hunting and find out how good they were. So he took his best lion dog and his two new dogs. They didn't go very far until a deer got up in front of them. One of those new dogs took off after it. So Dave got off his mule and shot this dog. A little farther up the trail another deer took off. The other new dog got after this deer. So Dave shot him, too.

Several months later Dave was back in Deming getting more supplies. He ran into the guy who gave him the dogs. "How are you getting along with your new lion dogs, Dave?"

Dave looked puzzled and asked, "What lion dogs are you talking about?"

"You know, those two dogs I gave you a few months ago?"

"Oh, those deer-running sons of bitches. I shot them both the first day!"

Dave was a great storyteller and a lot of fun to be with. Whenever he talked about someone he didn't like, he said he would like to buy them for what they were worth and sell them for what they thought they were worth and keep the difference!

Mexican mules.

Dave Spilsbury (right) with "Dos Amigos" and Mexico male lion.

'83 Flood

In October of '83, Joe Vander Hulst, a second cousin of mine, drew an antelope tag for Northern Arizona. He was 14 years old at the time. My dad, Joe's dad, Paul, and I went along to help on this hunt.

It rained all the way up to camp. It continued to rain the entire time we were there (3 days) - very unusual for our area. We did manage to find a good buck for Joe, and he killed his first antelope.

We wanted to spend some time up north and enjoy Northern Arizona. It is usually a great place to spend time in October. After the third day we decided to go home and dry out. It rained all the way home.

When we got to Marana (north of Tucson) there was about 2"-3" of water flowing across the freeway. I told dad it had to be the Santa Cruz River flooding its banks. He couldn't believe it. We turned on the radio to listen to the news. Southern Arizona was having a major flood. 100 year flood, they said.

Everyone was able to get home except me. All of the bridges in my area were washed out or closed. My mother was staying in our home baby-sitting for Allen, who was 6 months old at the time. My wife and daughter, Julie, were in New Mexico. In addition to the bridges being closed, all of the telephones in our area were out of service. I couldn't drive home or call home. I was concerned about mom and Allen.

I decided to call a friend and co-worker, Dave Graham, who lives in Tucson. I was hoping he could borrow an airplane to fly me home. (There is an airstrip behind my house that is owned and operated by F.I.C.O., the company I work for.) Dave told me to meet him at the Tucson Airport in one hour (9:00 PM). When we met, he informed me the only airplane he could borrow was a twin engine Cessna 402. I was hoping he could find a single engine airplane. We flew to Continental (20 miles) and made several low passes with the landing lights on to orient us to the runway. It was very dark and raining hard, and the runway lights were off. (Dave can fly an airplane better upside down than most people can fly right side up. I have a lot of confidence in his flying skills.) Dave made a good landing. However, the runway was standing in water. The airplane started to hydroplane. When Dave started braking, the left main tire blew out. It was quite a ride! Dave kept the airplane under control. We left it parked on the runway, and I walked home to see mom and Allen. All was well. They had food and water, electricity and heat. I offered them an airplane ride to Tucson. Mom declined. She told me to drive home whenever they opened a bridge.

I walked back to the airstrip to see what Dave's game plan was. He decided we would borrow a tire from the company Cessna 421, install it on the 402, and fly the airplane back to Tucson that night. We were very cold, wet, and tired by the time we finished. Dave taxied to the far North end of the runway. It was still raining hard and black as the inside of a cow. We turned the runway lights on and applied full power to both engines. The standing water on the airstrip was an added drag we didn't need. This short farm strip has an FAA approved 50 ft. tree on each end with a power line running parallel on the West side! It is a very marginal strip for a twin engine airplane not equipped with a STOL kit (short take off or landing flaps). The airplane staggered off the ground with the stall warning screaming in our ears. The fact that Dave and I are living today is testimony to the fact he is a highly skilled pilot.

After we landed in Tucson, I thanked Dave for his help and asked him what I owed him. He replied, "I would never make a trip like that for money. It's too dangerous! I did this as a favor to a friend." I didn't know how good a friend Dave was. I do now!

Joe Vander Hulst
Northern Arizona
1983

Pecan Orchard Attacks Border Patrol

By David Johnson

Enclosed are two articles copied from a local newspaper following an incident at the pecan farm I manage in Cochise County, Arizona. The incident occurred at 4:14 am on November 20, 2000.

Dragoon farm's bird scare cannons mistaken for real gunfire incident

Chris Dabovich - Arizona Range News

What authorities initially believed to be gunfire turned out to be measures taken strictly for the birds.

U.S. Border Patrol agents on Monday morning apparently mistook a propane-powered device used by some farmers to scare off birds. The incident occurred in Dragoon at about 4:15 a.m.

Dozens of officers converged on the area after receiving the report of shots fired. Benson Police officers, Cochise County Sheriff's Deputies and Arizona Department of Public Safety officers responded to provide assistance and Border Patrol agents returned fire.

U.S. Border Patrol spokesman Rob Daniels said because of an ongoing investigation, he could not provide specifics into the incident. "Until we complete our investigation, we are not at liberty to discuss the incident," Daniels said on Monday afternoon.

Cochise County Sheriff's Dept. spokeswoman Carol Capas said only that deputies responded to assist following the report of shots fired. She did say that deputies cleared the scene at about 6:30 a.m.

Authorities cordoned off Dragoon Road and embarked on a lengthy search for the perceived shooters.

The search, which included air surveillance, was called off more than two hours later when authorities determined the shots were actually fired from the scare gun.

David Johnson, manager of Sunland Farms, said seven scare guns have been operating at the farm's orchards around the clock for about two months. He said the devices are used to scare off "everything from ravens to javelina."

Johnson, who was not at the farm at the time of the incident, said he told an assistant manager to explain to the agents that the gunfire they heard was probably the "scare cannons."

What was concerning to Johnson, he said, was "they (border patrol) didn't tell anyone they were going to start shooting; they just did."

*****

Complaint filed against Border Patrol after 'shooting' incident

Chris Dabovich – Arizona Range News

A 65-year-old woman has filed a complaint with the Office of the Inspector General after she and a companion were forced from her vehicle at gunpoint by U.S. Border Patrol agents who accused the pair of shooting at them during the early-morning hours of Nov. 20.

The incident capped a day Border Patrol officials would soon like to forget and they are not commenting on the matter citing an ongoing investigation.

Meanwhile Emmy Selting, the woman stopped on the Interstate, remains livid a week after the ordeal.

"I'm furious," Selting said. "I feel so violated and I feel embarrassed. This was totally unjust and uncalled for and they're going to have to answer to that. I felt we were treated like criminals. I understand what they (Border Patrol) go through and the danger, but for me the whole thing is a very upsetting situation."

It all started shortly after 4 a.m. when Douglas-based Border Patrol agents reported they were being fired upon while patrolling in the Cochise area. Several law enforcement officers, Cochise County Sheriff's Dept. deputies, Arizona Department of Public Safety and Benson Police converged on the scene southwest of Willcox to assist the Border Patrol agents who returned fire.

A supervisory agent at the Douglas station on Nov. 20 would neither confirm nor deny that the incident had taken place.

Sheriff's investigators later determined that the reported shots were actually blasts from a propane-powered contraption used at

Sunland Farms to frighten away birds and other animals from nearby apple and pecan orchards.

The Border Patrol agents returned fire into the darkness. A Cochise County Sheriff's Dept. report stated that as deputies came upon three Border patrol vehicles, agents were observed firing their weapons toward the Sunland Farms orchard located on Cochise Stronghold Road between Dragoon and Sunsites.

"I had stopped my car and at the same time they were screaming like they do on the shows on television 'Get out of the car, put your hands on the roof.' Another officer screamed at me to put my hands behind my back. I said, 'Make up your cotton-picking mind.'"

As she walked backward, Selting said she was pushed up against the Border Patrol vehicle, frisked, and then forcefully handcuffed. She said that's when she saw all the guns pointed at her.

"I'm 5 feet 2 inches tall and weigh 140 pounds. I know they have to be careful. I'm a 65-year-old grandmother of four. I feel there should have been a quick and more accurate assessment on behalf of the Border Patrol officers," Selting said.

"I'm very proud of Emmy," husband Lehand said. "I told the Border Patrol that she didn't start anything but she will surely finish it." Lehand said a Border Patrol "liaison" asked if their home had sustained any bullet-hole damage. Lehand said their home was not hit.

The Seltings are not the only ones upset with the agency's apparent reckless abandon.

Earl Moser, of Willcox, who lives within a mile of where the incident occurred, said he is appalled by the agency's reaction.

"I could have been driving down that road," Moser said. "For them (agents) to fire into the orchard is totally irresponsible. I am really peeved. Basically their actions tell us that we're a danger and that's what is really upsetting," Moser said.

Rob Daniels, spokesman of the patrol's Tucson Sector, acknowledged last week a formal complaint was received from Selting but said because of the ongoing investigation he was not at liberty to comment.

One area resident said investigators spray painted circles on the road where empty shell casings were found. He said there were 29 painted circles.

Selting and companion, whom she identified only as a family friend, had the apparent misfortune of driving away from Cochise Stronghold Road shortly after the 4:15 a.m. incident.

Selting and friend were en route to Tucson. Selting explained she takes two weekly trips to the city and usually leaves between 4 and 4:30 a.m. Selting had no prior knowledge of the "shots fired" incident that occurred just north of her home.

By the time deputies had determined no shots had been fired, Selting and friend had been put through the ordeal she still describes as "infuriating."

"I'm still furious," Selting, originally from Germany, said last week. "They (Border Patrol agents) never identified themselves and never told me what this was all about. It was like Hitler and the Gestapo. I fled East Germany during World War II and I've been shot at many times during the war. The thing with the Border Patrol did not frighten me. I felt furious. I have had two heart attacks and that night I felt pains in my chest. When I get seriously upset I get pains in my chest. I'm not supposed to be stressed. They never did tell me exactly why they stopped me. All they said was "You shot at us."

Her denials were ignored, Selting said while noting she and her friend were detained for about half an hour.

While pulled over on the interstate, east of Benson, Selting said she and her companion were handcuffed and frisked and put into Border Patrol vehicles.

Authors Note: A special thanks to Sunland Farm Manager, David Johnson, for providing this information for this book.

Mexico Border Lion

Terry and John Bessett are both good friends of mine and are also good hunters. John has hunted lions with Ollie and has shot a big trophy tom and one or two smaller ones. Terry wanted a lion real bad. We traded some plumbing work for a lion hunt.

On one occasion the dogs were trailing up a canyon. They were going real slow. It started to rain a little, but the dogs kept going. I made a mistake on this hunt I won't repeat. We had tied up the horses to walk down the bluff 50 yards or so to see what the dogs were doing. We left the rifle in the scabbard. All of a sudden a big tom lion jumped up on a rock 25 yards or so right below us! And no gun! I whispered to Terry, "Go fetch the 30-30." By the time he got back, the lion had left, and with the rain, the dogs were unable to trail it up again.

The next time we caught a lion for Terry, Ollie and Tom Barkley (a good friend of Ollie and I), and I were hunting along the Mexican Border when the dogs trailed a lion up in some big rocks. The lion wasn't really caught, but we could see it plain. It was a long, hard shot for my 30-30; Terry missed and the lion ran off. It was in terrible country with big boulders and the lion got away in the rocks.

When we finally did catch Terry his lion, we were back along the Mexican Border. We were camped out at an old ranch and were going to hunt several days. The first day the dogs trailed almost all morning up and down the canyon. We could see lion sign where the dogs were going backwards at least part of the time. Finally, one of our best dogs we call "Sally" trailed up on top of a rocky peak. The other dogs didn't know where she went. When she got out of hearing, we rimmed around to try to locate her. What a sight! She had a big trophy tom caught all by herself on a big rock! She was nose to nose with this lion.

We rode as far as we could and tied up our mounts. Terry and I climbed up to where he could get a shot. We could hear Sally barking, but the lion moved and we couldn't figure out where it was. We kept climbing around, and all of a sudden we saw the lion. It was crouched down and trying to hide. It wasn't 15 yards away! Terry shot and the lion ran right past me. I didn't see a spot of blood. Sally was right on his tail when he left. "Terry, I think you missed!" "I don't think I did," replied Terry. In a minute we could hear Sally barking again. We climbed down to where she was. The lion was dead. It was a real big male lion, big enough to get into the Arizona Record Book. We tied the lion on a horse we call "River" and Terry walked back to camp and led the horse. He was one happy camper, proving once again that the third time truly is a charm. Ollie and I were both real happy that Terry got such a good lion.

Note: River was a registered Quarter horse. When we bought him "Liki" Felix and Allen trained him for calf roping and team roping. When Allen stopped roping, I started using him for lion hunting. He was one of the smartest and best all around horses I have ever seen.

Terry Bessett's lion
with River, Terry Bessett and Ollie Barney.

Roos and Cockatoos

In 1995 I had the good fortune to visit the land down under. The company I work for, F.I.C.O., and the Stahmann family have been friends for many years. Keith Walden, the founder of F.I.C.O., had all of the pecan trees in Arizona grown in Stahmann's nursery in Las Cruces, New Mexico. Deane Stahmann, Jr. developed a pecan orchard in Moree, New South Wales, Australia in the early '70's. He was doing some interesting work with pruning pecan trees that F.I.C.O. was very interested in seeing. Keith Walden and I decided to make the trip down there in June to have a look around. Unfortunately, Keith sprained his ankle a week before we were scheduled to leave. He decided not to make the trip, so I went solo.

The 19 hour plane trip from Los Angeles to Sydney was uneventful. I marveled at modern technology - 500+ miles per hour, non-stop for 19 hours, carrying God knows how much weight! I spent the night in Sydney and traveled the next day to Brisbane. I sat next to an attractive local lady with 2 small children. When I told her I was in Australia to visit a pecan orchard, she told me she didn't know what pecans were. After describing them to her, she exclaimed, "Oh, we call them peckens! I make a pecken pie every Christmas." I began to understand why marketing pecans was so difficult. In Australia they call pecans "peckens", in the U.S. East of the Mississippi they call them "peecans", and West of the Mississippi they call them "pecans".

In Brisbane I boarded a commuter flight to Toowoomba (the garden city). I rented a car there to drive the 200± miles to the farm in Moree. It was a very strange feeling driving on the left side of the road from the right side of the car. I did fine in the country. I noticed they give you the finger in the city, the same as back home!

The trip to Moree was relaxing and interesting. I've never seen so many different kinds of birds. I wondered if ravens are on every continent on planet earth!

I was met at the farm by the owner, Deane Stahmann. He was a great host, and we enjoyed one another's company very much. I wished Keith could have made the trip. We spent several days talking about pecans and sharing what we have learned over the years. Deane was also interested in the macadamia business. If I would have had more time, I would have enjoyed learning more about that industry. Deane is a true pioneer and a damned good pecan farmer.

I told Deane I sure wanted to shoot a kangaroo while I was there. (Roos, as they are called by the locals.) He introduced me to Rick Hancock, who works for the farm during the day and hunts roos at night. At dusk he picked me up in his Nissan 4x4 pickup, and we went hunting. He had a roof mounted spotlight and a stainless .223 Ruger with a 6x Leopold scope. We hunted in an area that was planted to winter wheat, and the plants were about 4" high. The wheat is all grown without irrigation, but so far the rains had been favorable.

Rick would hold the spotlight on the roos and I would line the cross hairs up with their eyeballs. They would drop like a sack of potatoes. I shot several species of roos and a Black Wallaroo and an Australian hare. Great fun! Rick skins and quarters the roos and stores them in his freezer at home. Once a month a truck from a dog food manufacturing plant in Sydney picks up the meat and pays him so much per pound. I inquired if they were good to eat. He claimed they were better than beef.

The next day Deane asked if I would like to participate in a cockatoo shoot. I was excited. They explained how this hunt would take place. They round up the pecan eating pests with a Piper Cub aircraft and herd the birds into an area where the shooters would be. The only word of caution was "Don't shoot the airplane!" When they found out I was a pilot, they invited me to fly the airplane. I declined, stating I would rather do some shooting. After I shot the first bird, I began to wonder if I shot the right species. It was a big beautiful snow white bird with a yellow crest on its head. I imagined it would sell for a $1,000.00 in a pet shop in the U.S.! I asked another shooter if this was what we were hunting for. He answered in the affirmative. I commented, "I don't know if I can shoot something as pretty as this." He said, "Don't worry. If you can't, we will. These S.O.B.'s are eating all of our profits!" On the strength of that, I resumed shooting.

I thoroughly enjoyed my first trip to the land down under. I hope to return some day and spend more time. I enjoyed the people, their accents, the food, the wildlife, the countryside, and the hospitality of everyone I met.

The trip home was also uneventful. However, 15 hours is a long time to sit with 2 lesbians on a crowded 747!

I feel fortunate to work for a company that would send me halfway around the world to look at pecan trees.

Author with roos, Australia, 1995.

Author with cockatoos, Australia, 1995.

Javelina in a Tree

By Ollie Barney

In all of my years of hunting lions and other game in Southern Arizona (over 50 years), I have only once seen where a lion killed a javelina and dragged it into a tree.

Several years after Michael Braeglemann and I found one in a tree on the Elkhorn Ranch, I was visiting with Warner Glenn from Southeastern Arizona at a mutual friend's house, Sewell Goodwin. He told me he saw the same thing one time. He theorized that after the lion killed the javelina, the other javelina gave the lion such a bad time that he ran up a tree to get away from the other pigs and took his kill with him. It stands to reason that's probably what happened. It was a very unusual thing to see.

Javelina in tree with Maggie inspecting.

George Parker's Lion

By Ollie Barney

This story is about a lion hunt I made with my good friend, George Parker, probably one of the better hunters in the world, who had hunted everywhere and on a limited budget, but he always managed to get in on the good places at the right time and make some real hunts. He had tried to get a mountain lion, he told me, since he was about 10 years old. One of his uncles was a government hunter and every chance he'd get, he'd go out with this uncle, but, as luck would have it, the uncle never could catch a lion while George was along. This went on, he said, he'd been huntin' a lion for 52 years – that's a long time to get a lion. So I told him to keep his eyes open for a good lion track somewhere and we'd see what we could do about catchin' it.

Several months later George called me and he said, "Ollie, I have just found the biggest lion track I ever saw in my life, right down here in Amado, right in my front yard." So I said I'd get things squared away and come down and we'd see if we could catch him. He says, "Ollie, this track is so big, it could be a jaguar!"

This was in the early '70s – I forget exactly what year it was. I went down and we made our hunt and the first day we made a few circles in there and cut all the sand washes and places we could, 'cause I wanted to see the tracks. And we found 'em – we found this track in a sand wash there on the Sopori Ranch. I got down and checked it out and I says, "George, this isn't a jaguar tract – it's a lion track, but it *is* one of the bigger lion tracks I ever saw." He wanted to know if I was sure it wasn't a jaguar and I told him I was no authority on jaguar tracks, "but you know we saw some in Venezuela in the mud and they track different from a mountain lion." I says, "You know, they're so much heavier in the front and narrow behind – their front tracks are wider apart than their hind tracks and then the hind tracks will be alongside of the front tracks and generally they'll overstep with their hind feet and then they'll be slightly in front."

A lion always steps with his hind foot in his front track when he's walkin' along, but I have seen where a lion walkin' down a sand wash will overstep a little too, but generally their hind track is right in their front track. You have to see it in wet sand before you can see where it will be off just a little bit – won't be exactly in it, but it will be awfully close.

And we went on and hunted for four or five days there and got one good run one day – the dogs were workin' real good, and we finally found a track after we had trailed it for a couple of hours, but it was a female track. We pulled the dogs off then 'cause George just wanted that one big trophy Tom.

We hunted along for a year – just short hunts – for a total of 17 days and no lion, but we pulled the dogs off of several female tracks and several kitten tracks, and there was a lesser Tom in there that we had seen the tracks of, but never did ever find one that the dogs could work or we'd atried to get it. George wasn't so fussy that he had to have the *biggest* lion in the State of Arizona.

Well, we went along and the word kinda leaked out about this big lion bein' in there, and Clay Howell, he went in there with Chuck Westenburg and they caught this lesser Tom. They thought they might have got the big one, but George saw it and he knew it wasn't the big lion. So he called me and he said, "Ollie, you got to get down here – we got to get workin' on this big lion before someone else catches it 'cause the word is out." All lion hunters always got their ears to the ground for an extra big lion. Some of 'em, like myself, it don't even have to be too big a one to want to get in there and try to catch it.

So I went down there and this bein' the 18th day ahuntin', we made a circle in there and along the afternoon we came to a big sand wash and there was a buzzard and a raven flew out. I says, "George, there's somethin' dead in there." We went down and of course by the time we got there, the dogs had already been there and opened on a lion track, and we found a calf killed there on the Sopori Ranch. We checked the tracks around there and sure enough it's the big lion – the calf had been buried back there alongside the bank, but coyotes had drug it out. We called the dogs off 'cause it was too late in the afternoon to try to catch the lion and I didn't want to excite him if he was layin' around where he could hear the dogs and keep him from comin' back that night.

The next mornin' we got in there real early – in fact, a few minutes before daylight, and we had to wait awhile before we could see tracks. 'Course the dogs knew right where the kill was, and hell, soon as they got out they ran down there and opened up and then the dogs split up. Three of 'em headed out northeast and crossed a hill covered with grass and brush, and the two other dogs – the older ones – they turned up a big wash aheadin' towards this Diablo Mountain some 2 ½ or 3 miles away. I told George, I says, "Hell, part of these dogs are on a backtrack but I think I can find the track ahead of the two dogs in the sand wash," and I went up there and sure enough, they were on the big lion and they were right. By that time the younger dogs was too far off to call back or to even catch, and I told George, "Hell, these two dogs can catch him."

So we followed 'em and the old lion, he meandered around all over the country. He'd come into this kill pretty early in the night – generally, they'll come in later – from 3:00 o'clock 'til daylight. Anyway this has been my experience. We went up on the north side of this Diablo Mountain and we followed as far as we could ahorseback and tied our horses, and the dogs climbed out on the east side of Diablo and trailed around the east side of the mountain. The track was hard to follow and George was ahavin' a little trouble akeepin' up and finally the dogs bayed this lion – they never jumped it at all. They was just acold-trailin' and then started abayin' right out on the edge of a high bluff – oh, a bluff maybe a hundred foot high. I eased down there and hell, the lion was out on a little ledge and the dogs was abarkin' right in his face and wasn't over two feet away from him. The old lion would hiss and slap at 'em and when he would hiss, they'd back off and the lion couldn't catch hold of 'em. They was pretty smart old dogs anyway – they didn't want to be caught by a lion of that size. I backed off where I wouldn't excite the lion and got George's attention and motioned him on down there. 'Course he could hear the dogs abayin' and he was ahurryin' right along. When he got down to me, I said, "George, now this lion is out on a little ledge right in front of the dogs. If you're not careful you'll be lookin' over the top of him and not seein' him 'cause he's partially hid there." He eased up there and sure enough he couldn't see the lion – he was alookin' over the top of him. Pretty soon that thing hissed and slapped at a dog and the dogs fell back and the lion boiled out of there. If he'd a hit George he'd a knocked him down, 'cause, God, he went right by him. Probably with the leap he made out of there, he coulda hit George in the shoulder and if George'd been along the edge of the bluff, he coulda knocked him off. That's one thing you always have to watch for when you've got a lion in the bluffs – that the damn thing don't knock you off. I've had several of 'em jump right by me and one that jumped clear over me.

Anyway, this lion baled off in a deep canyon there and come out on the other side about 75 yards from George and arunnin' fast. George got off one shot at it and hit it in the front part of the stomach just in back of the liver. The dogs took it on around the south end of Diablo Mountain probably 600-700 yards and bayed it in another bluffy little canyon. When we got up there all we could see was the lion's head and see him slap at a dog once in a while. George was maneuverin' around tryin' to find a place where he could shoot it in the neck or the shoulder 'cause he didn't want to ruin the skull.

Pretty soon this lion caught Lucky – just sucked her in and bit her right in the base of the skull and dropped her after he bit her. She just dropped like she was dead and I thought she *was* dead. I says, "George, one of us has got to kill this lion or he's gonna kill both dogs and then get away." Well, George jumped right down and stuck his rifle up where he thought was the neck and pulled the trigger. He shot off a little bit of the back part of the skull, but fortunately there was enough of the base of the skull left so we could get an accurate measurement. It made the Boone & Crockett Book and this was the only lion that I've ever caught that made Boone & Crockett. I was sure glad that George got it 'cause he has all kinds of trophies in Boone & Crockett, in the Safari Club Book and the Arizona Book, and he was quite conscious of trophy animals.

Then the dogs just baled right onto this lion as soon as it dropped and they rolled down over a bluff about 10 foot high. George had his bird dog along – Old Bandit he called him – and Bandit, he really got excited. He was tryin' to tear that lion to shreds and of course George was proud of him. Finally, Lucky come to and then she jumped into the fracas and mauled the lion – we let 'em maul it for a few minutes and then we called 'em off and gutted the lion out and George took a picture or two. We split the pelvis – took everything out of it we could and drained it good. Then we got some dry grass and wiped out all the blood inside and got it as dry as we could, because this was the day before Easter and it was pretty warm. There was no goin' back that day 'cause, hell, we had about a 3-mile ride ahorseback and another 2 ½ miles to get to the horses afoot and this was terribly rough country and slow goin' and it was already by then 3:30. We got back to the horses and when you get out and make one of these hikes in hot weather, you're always glad to get back to your horses. We rode on back to the truck and trailer and the other 3 dogs was there. I'm sure that they had tracked another lion and caught it, but bein' young dogs they'd probably stayed with it four or five hours and then quit it. I know there was two lions 'cause the big lion had been in a fight there over the kill. He had several pretty good cuts on him and scratches made by another lion who must have been a salty damn lion to take on a lion as big as this one was. I guess they're like some men – they'll take on more than they can handle sometimes.

We got our horses loaded and it was well after dark when we got back down to George's place in Amado. In the morning we took a pack mule and went around on the southeast side of Diablo Mountain, managed to get this pack mule up to the lion and loaded it and brought it out. We took it down to George's and weighed it – it weighed 135 pounds. With it fairly well drained out and everything peeled out of it, I imagine it woulda weighed another 15 or 20 pounds with the bait of the calf he had in him.

This was the biggest lion that I ever caught – weight-wise and in measurement of the skull, and it couldn't have gone to a better guy than my good friend, George Parker.

Ollie on Smokie

Southern Arizona, 1993

Photo by Tony King

Sonoita Creek Lion

Several years ago, I got a phone call from a rancher in Sonoita Creek. A lion had killed a calf; it was in the middle of summer. It had been over 100 degrees every day. Conditions would be extremely difficult to catch the lion. Being sympathetic to ranchers, I agreed to try.

Rocky Lopez, the head mechanic at F.I.C.O., wanted to shoot a lion. He had never hunted with me before. I told him to be at my house at 3:00 a.m. and we would drive down to the ranch and have a look around.

We met the rancher and rode down to the kill. The lion had come in early and finished off the baby calf and left. The dogs tried trailing in every direction, but couldn't find a track good enough to trail. I looked around but I couldn't find where the lion left. There were not many places to see a track, and the dogs had left tracks everywhere.

I told the rancher I couldn't help him, and we started back to camp. We rode up the bottom of the canyon towards the Patagonia Lake Dam. We were almost to the dam when the dogs threw their heads up and ran into a thicket of trees and brush. In a minute they were barking treed! I looked around and saw lots of coon tracks. I'd never seen my dogs tree a coon before, but I was sure they had today. I told Rocky to get the rifle, and we would go into this thicket and shoot this coon. After crawling on our hands and knees a short distance, we got to a place where we could see. The dogs had an adult female lion treed! I was sure surprised. Rocky made a good shot and the rancher was as surprised as I was to see us dragging this lion. It was one of the easiest hunts I've ever been on. I was happy for the rancher, Rocky, and my hounds. This lion was not the calf killer. We checked her and she did not have any calf hair in her stomach. The rancher was happy nonetheless. This is the only time I have caught a lion without trailing it up. Rocky had hunted lions for a total of about 2 hours. He is one of my luckier hunters. Much luckier than his brother Juan!

Rocky Lopez with Sonoita Creek lion.

Pinta's First Puma

Pinta was 6 months old when I took her lion hunting for the first time. Ray McGee called me and said that he had a client who wanted to shoot a mountain lion with a bow and arrow. I had heard of a big tom making sign on John King's "King's Anvil Ranch" south of Three Points. We made plans to make a one-day hunt to have a look around.

We left Green Valley at 3:00 a.m. and picked Ray's client up at 3:30 in Tucson. We met Ken Lange from the Elkhorn Ranch at 4:30. As soon as we could see the trail, we headed for the mountain. We didn't get very far when Ray and I realized that his client could not ride a horse well enough in those mountains without hurting himself, or the horse. Ray and I had a short confidential "Board of Directors" meeting. We decided that he would go back to camp with his client and I would continue on with Ken and make a "short" hunt.

We rode to the mountain summit and followed a good trail south towards the Elkhorn Ranch. When the dogs came to a low saddle ahead of us, they stated to work a track. Trailing conditions were not very good, but they were able to trail it into the timber. The only dogs I had were Sally (Pinta's mother), Ike (½ hound and ½ Catahoula), and Pinta (Ollie Barney and I are partners on 7 dogs, including the 3 I had on this hunt). The dogs only trailed for about ¼ of a mile or so until I heard them jump the lion out. They didn't go far until they were treed. When Pinta heard them barking treed, she went to them. Before Ken and I could get to the tree, the lion jumped out and went over the mountain. It was too rough for the horses, so we had to go on foot. When we got to the top, we could hear them bark treed again. But, before we could even see the lion, he jumped out a 2nd time. They ran this lion a long ways and finally stopped him in some big high bluffs. Ken climbed up and shot the lion with his pistol. The lion fell a long ways.

I took Pinta down so she could see her 1st lion. She was a little intimidated with the size. He was a big trophy male. It was then that we realized it was getting late in the day. We decided to leave the lion. Ken said that he and some other cowboys would pick it up the next day. The moon came up at about the same time the sun went down so we could see pretty well. I had to stop and rest several times with cramps in my legs. I thought I was gonna have to spend the night in those mountains. We finally made it to our horses and we arrived at the Elkhorn Ranch at about 9:00 p.m. Bob Miller, Ray, and his client were getting pretty worried. I called my wife and Bob fed us dinner with his usual hospitality. Ken and I were very tired and hungry. The dogs were give out and they laid up in the mountains. By the time we ate, loaded our horses, and drove home it was midnight. I had been gone on a one-day hunt for 21 hours.

The dogs showed up at John King's Ranch and I picked them up the following day. I don't know of another sport that can be more exhausting or more gratifying.

Pinta is now 3 years old and has been in on more than 20 lions and 7 bears. I am proud of her. Ollie and I will see to it that she has a good home for as long as she lives.

My son Allen was 14 at the time and I expect Pinta will be teaching him to hunt lions soon.

Ken Lange (left) with Ollie and trophy male lion packed out on Ollie's mule, Smokey.

Two For The Price of One

I became acquainted with a well driller in Eastern Arizona by the name of Talbott Starlings. He had done quite a little hunting. He asked if I would catch him a lion. I told him I would take him hunting and the only thing I would guarantee him was a sore ass.

I called him one September evening and I told him I was going to make a little circle Sunday morning if he wanted to join me.

I took some of Brian Thomas' dogs and some of mine and Ollie's dogs. We drove for about thirty minutes from my house to the Tumacacori Mountains. It was still dark riding up the jeep trail when we left camp. A dog we call Bell started a track. It was slow going, but she did get the other dogs interested. They were all trailing real slow. They finally trailed over a little ridge. As they trailed over the ridge we could hear the track getting a lot better. I told Talbott, "We have got a good chance to catch a lion today." I hardly got the words out of my mouth when the dogs started barking treed. We tied up our horses and walked over to where the dogs were. This lion was high in a big oak tree. It was still kind of dark, but we could see the lion plain. Talbott borrowed my .44 magnum rifle and shot. The tree shook and the lion never moved. He shot twice more with the same results. "Talbott, we better get a little different angle on this lion. I don't want to drive all the way to Tucson for more bullets!" There was a big limb we couldn't see with all of the leaves in the way. When we moved a few yards, he made a good clean kill. We had been hunting less than an hour.

While we were tying this lion on his horse, the dogs started trailing back the way they came. "What are those dogs doing now?" asked Talbott. "I think they are back trailing," I said. "They will do that sometimes just to entertain themselves." In just a few minutes, they started barking treed again. When I told Talbott they had another lion caught, he was really surprised. So was I. It was another grown female lion, the same size as the one he had just shot. Apparently these young lions (littermates) were still traveling together. We put dog chains on the dogs and led them away from the tree. In doing so, we found where the lions had just killed a whitetail doe. I'm sure they were feeding on this deer when the dogs trailed them up.

Talbott thinks lion hunting is easy. I'll have to take him on a real hunt someday!

Talbott Starlings with female lion.

Santa Rita Ranch Calf Killer

A neighboring rancher and friend called me one day in May complaining of losing calves to lion depredation. He had a Phoenix hunter come out and hunt a few days without any luck. I told George Burruel I would hunt the first chance I got. One Sunday morning, Buck Garner, a friend of mine who also hunts lions, and my brother, Dale, and I left my house at 3:00 a.m. We trailered to the Santa Rita Ranch in Sawmill Canyon. When it got light enough to see, we hit the trail. We rode into a low saddle behind Bill McGibbons' house. We had three trained dogs and three young dogs. (Buck had a couple of young dogs and I had a couple of mine and Ollie's dogs, and I borrowed a couple of dogs from Brian Thomas.) When the dogs hit the saddle, the old dogs hit a good track. One dog we call Major, trailed up on the mountain and all the rest of the dogs trailed down country. With all the dog tracks and cow tracks I couldn't find a lion track, so I didn't know which end of the track was right. In a few minutes, I could hear Major high on the mountain. The sound was faint, but he sounded like he was treed. I listened awhile longer. I was convinced he was treed. The other dogs were going on the back track. I jogged down to where they were on my mule and stopped them. I took the dogs back up to where they could hear Major. When they did, they built to him in a hurry. We rode as far as we could then tied up our mules. The dogs were all barking treed, and they had a real nice male lion treed. Dale made a good shot. After the lion hit the ground the dogs chewed on it for a while. We loaded the lion onto Buck's mule and headed for the ranch to water the dogs. We unloaded the lion there and rode to camp to get the trucks and trailers. I checked the lions stomach and it was full of calf hair and meat. George was sure happy that we caught the calf killer. He had been causing lots of problems. Dale was real happy with his lion.

Bill McGibbon and George Burruel are good friends and good ranchers. Bill has served several terms as a State Representative for our area. He has been a lot of help on hunting, farming and ranching issues. We need more people like Bill, who understand the issues, representing us in Arizona and in the U.S. Senate.

Dale Brandt with male lion and mule, Helen.
(Buck's mule)

Picnics and Pumas

I had tried off and on for several years to catch a lion for a good friend of mine, Juan Lopez, Sr. He was not very lucky. On several occasions, I had called him to go hunting and something would come up and he couldn't go. On some of those days I caught several good lions. Whenever Juan was along, we struck out. My average is a lion for every 10 days of hunting. When I was hunting with Juan, my average wasn't that good, or at least it seemed that way!

The deal was, when we started hunting, that he would supply the burritos. His wife, Ernestina, is a wonderful cook and really makes a mean burrito! I was really enjoying our picnics! Juan finally concluded that I didn't want to catch him a lion! He claimed, if I caught him a lion, I would go hungry! He decided to bring peanut butter sandwiches instead. Maybe that would motivate me to catch him a lion. That didn't work either! I just couldn't catch a lion when Juan was along! But we enjoyed our picnics and one another's company (I think).

After several years of hunting on and off, I was still trying to catch Juan a lion.

One evening a friend and neighboring rancher, Ray McGee, called. His dad had found a calf killed by a lion that day. It was in August and hot as hell. He asked if I could try to catch it. I am always sympathetic to ranchers. However, I had commitments the next day I couldn't get out of. I told him I would loan him my truck and trailer and a horse and three dogs to try to catch it, with one condition. I wanted him to invite Juan. I felt they had a good chance of catching it.

They left real early the next morning, and were at the kill by 5 a.m. The dogs took the track and left in a hurry and were out of hearing in no time. They only had one horse, so Ray left Juan at the kill and followed the dogs. When Ray caught up with them, they were just milling around and were real hot. Ray watered the dogs. After the dogs were cooled down, Ray decided to have a look around. By chance he looked up and saw the lion in the tree! He was as hot as the dogs! Ray picked up a young dog we called "Red" and showed him the lion. He just got stiff and started barking. He was excited. On the strength of that, the other dogs joined in. Ray jogged back to get Juan and they rode double back to the lion, and Juan shot the Big Trophy male lion.

On this hunt my telephone was my best strike dog and Ray

was my best tree dog! Ray did a great job under very harsh conditions.

Juan is still not convinced I am a good lion hunter, but I'm convinced his wife is one of the best cooks in Southern Arizona!

Juan Lopez with record book lion

Old Hunting Dog

Beryl J. Barney

This poem was written by Ollie's late wife, Beryl J. Barney. It was written about one of Ollie's favorite hounds, Drifter. These poems (along with others) were published in the American Poetry Anthology, Volume VIII, number five.

Beryl was a dear friend of ours for many years. She passed away in 1995. Our son, Allen, looked up to Beryl as a step-grandmother. She was a sweet and kind person who was loved by all who knew her. Beryl's 4 children gave me permission to reprint the poems used in my book.

He sleeps on the doormat, dreaming
Of chasing a cougar through the snow,
His stomach is quivering, legs moving jerkily
And a moan comes softly from his throat.

He was the hero of one hundred chases,
Shrewd and gifted leader of the pack.
His nose was like a Geiger counter, checking
Until he finds the scent and takes the track.

Leading the other dogs to tree the lion
And hold it there until master comes.
And after the guided hunter takes his trophy
He swells with pride when his master says,
 "Well done!"

But now he is old and the ills of age are telling
On legs no longer strong as once they were,
The voice that bayed
 The hunters' favorite music
Is fading now and pain has stilled the burr

Faithful old dog, dream on and tree your lion.
You will be missed
 More than you'll ever know.
When you are gone
The hunt will be diminished
But memory will keep your feats aglow.

Beryl J. Barney
1917 - 1995

Lucky Wetback

Allen and I were lion hunting not far from the Mexican border one Sunday morning. All of a sudden we heard a man yelling. I told Allen to stay put. I took my .30-.30 out of the scabbard and put it across my lap. I didn't know what to expect. I didn't know if we stumbled into a drug deal, or if someone was hurt, or something else. I rode up cautiously, ready to dismount and use my horse for a shield if need be. When I got to the man, I saw he was a lost wetback. I visited with him in Spanish and told Allen to come down to us. The wetback was trying to get to Tucson through the mountains. It was in the summer and over 100° every day. I told him he would never make it alive. I told him how to get to the highway, and Allen and I gave him all of our food and water. If he took our advice, we saved his life. If he didn't, the coyotes ate him. He was hot and tired and his feet were bleeding. He was only wearing Mexican sandals. We also told him to travel at night and rest in the shade during the day. There are hundreds of wetbacks that die every year in the Southwest from heat exhaustion. I hope we saved one.

In the area where we live we see wetbacks almost daily. We all help them with food and water. We never turn them in to the Border Patrol. I feel sorry for the poor souls trying to improve their lives and that of their families. If I lived under the conditions most of them do, I'd be headed North, too.

A good friend of mine, Les Hanes, worked for the Border Patrol. He was flying a Cessna 182 and his luck ran out. He hit a power line and has gone to the happy hunting grounds. He always encouraged me to call him whenever I saw wetbacks. I told him I never would. We remained friends in spite of our philosophical differences.

Big Moose – Big Lion

By Bob Cheever

Growing up in Wyoming, most boys were introduced to hunting at a young age. Layne and I discovered that we both learned about hunting at our father's side.

From about the time I was in the 3rd grade, I would take off with my slingshot after school to see what I could find. I walked along the railroad tracks and would take aim at doves or other easy targets. In 4th grade, I sold Cloverine salve door to door and saved enough money to buy a Red Tyder BB gun. My family frequently spent summers and Sundays near the farming community of Carr, Colorado, where my mother's family lived. There I could find jack rabbits and snakes and other creatures to hunt.

By the time I was in 7th grade, I was allowed to go hunting with my father and three older brothers. Initially I wasn't allowed to use a gun, but went along to camp out, usually in the fall or early winter. We often hunted in the Snowy Range and near Encampment in Wyoming.

During elk hunting season, we might miss a week of school to hunt. Since my brothers and I went with Dad, we often had to share what guns were available. My Uncle Mark, who made a hobby of refurbishing old military guns from World War II, helped supply us. Dad had a pump action .22 rifle, a 12-gauge double-barrel shotgun and two 30.06 rifles. Mom might go on a weekend hunting trip, and she used a single shot .22. Usually she only enjoyed target shooting.

Dad was a good shot; if he saw the game, he usually got it. The animal was always taken back to Cheyenne to a meat processor and prepared to be frozen and eaten later. Mom was very adept at cooking wild meat.

When I was 15, I got drawn for moose. Our hunting group consisted of Dad, my brothers, Theo and KayDon, and me. After arriving near the Upper Green River in Wyoming, I paired off with Dad. We had settled down on the side of a mountain to have a snack, and just as we got up and started to walk towards the trees, a moose stood up. Dad handed me a military rifle on a sling and told me to take a shot. When I asked where to aim, he said, "take a head shot". And I did, and the moose went down.

Although we were close to camp, it took us 2 ½ days to move this 1400 pound animal. To accomplish this, we quartered him and took him out on poles. As we worked, we saw another moose watching us.

After our return home, I was photographed with the moose head by the local paper and the Denver Post. It was said that this moose was the biggest one shot in that area.

My first elk-hunting trip to Jackson Hole occurred the following year. A man who rented the shop behind us, Jack Gaudern, took me with him. For the first time, we used horses for hunting, and I took my own horse, Trixie, with me.

Many years later, in 1972, I moved with my family to Tucson, Arizona, where I met Layne Brandt at Farmers Investment Co. near Green Valley. For a time Layne was working there, then went to work in Tucson, and later came back to Farmers Investment and worked as shop foreman. I sold automotive parts and called on the shop every week. I learned that Layne was from Laramie, Wyoming and that he loved hunting. After my weekly sales call, Layne invited me to share lunch and then out to help him check traps that he had set. During these years, he allowed my brother, Roland, and me to keep our horses on the farm. Layne later became Vice President of Farmers Investment Co. and earned a reputation for being an accomplished big game hunter in Arizona.

A few years ago, Layne invited me to go along with him to hunt mountain lions. Layne had several horses and his dogs were trained to track the lions. River was the name of the horse that I enjoyed riding the most. At different times we would hunt in different mountain areas, some extremely steep and unapproachable unless on horseback. That was such a fantastic experience to climb on horseback into such isolated and sometimes treacherous areas with tremendous views only seen by a few persons. I always thought, as I sat up there on horseback, this is an experience no amount of money could buy. I wished often that I could bring my son, Cory, up there with me. What a wonderful experience it was to be allowed to share.

We sometimes had other hunters along with us. Buck from Nogales, who was a roofing contractor, often hunted from a mule, which is a more sure-footed animal and with greater endurance. John Bessett, a home builder from Green Valley, also came along at times. Layne's son, Allen, an accomplished hunter himself and blessed with a good eye for spotting game, was always an asset to the hunt. We also hunted with Ray McGee, from Sierrita Mining and Ranching, east of Green Valley. Ray's story of his family settling in Arizona on the way to find gold in California is very fascinating. They broke down in Arizona and ultimately decided to settle in that beautiful country (now called McGee Ranch).

Hunting with Layne always started in the early morning hours, and we loaded the horses and dogs in the dark. We would drive together in the cab and invariably talk about our youth and hunting with our fathers. Layne could describe his hunting experiences so clearly, making it easy to visualize.

On one occasion we (along with Ollie Barney) got permission to stay at a ranch that was not currently occupied. This was close to the Mexico border where many immigrant trails were visible. Layne warned me to acknowledge any immigrants we may meet, but then to turn around and head the other direction. If not, we risked their fear of law enforcement, and our safety would be in jeopardy. On one occasion, in this same general area, we saw through binoculars that people were climbing up a park ranger's lookout; another time we saw a green garbage bag, which Layne suggested probably held marijuana and said that we best ignore it.

Layne credits Ollie Barney with getting him interested in lion hunting and teaching him the key elements of the hunt. Layne's reputation as a lion hunter later attracted ranchers who would call him when they had lost calves to the mountain lions.

I have great admiration for Layne as a professional hunter, so very knowledgeable, and with excellent horses and dogs. The dogs are solely trained for lion hunting, and will not be distracted by deer, rabbits, javelina or other wildlife. The dogs are fitted with tracking collars. Layne uses an antenna to pick up their signal which allows the hunter to be guided by the dogs. There were times when the dogs picked up an old scent and then couldn't find the lions because they were too far away by then. But, it was obvious when they were on a fresh trail, their excitement was apparent from their howling. The dogs would "tree" the lion at the base of a tree or trap it up on a cliff.

Sometimes Layne and I had to wait on the dogs to return to our base. One Saturday we were up on the side of a mountain on the horses and tracking the dogs; we had 2 of Layne and Ollie's dogs and 1 of Chuck Lange's. When the dogs were located, we took off after them. Layne had inadvertently laid the control box on the ground, and this was not discovered until we were back to the horse trailer. We decided we would return the next day to retrieve the box.

On the ride back in, Layne spotted fresh tracks. He was adept at determining by the tracks whether it was a Tom or female, and how old the tracks were. We heard the dogs, and Layne said, "There should be a lion up there." We went to the base of the mountain and got off the horses and crawled about 125 yards along the ravine. We spotted the dogs, and Layne saw the lion up in a tree. I looked through the scope and saw the cat. Layne suggested I just sit and relax, and take my time before taking a shot. I decided I would take my Dad's advice of so many years before, and I took a head shot. Layne asked why I shot there, "that is the smallest target". I told him it was the same place I had shot my moose.

The lion dropped a great distance, and Layne commented, "If the shot didn't get him, the fall surely did". We rode the horses down and back up again to get the cat. I took the cat out lying across my lap on horseback. Ron McGinnis, the taxidermist, had hunted with me and another friend in the past, so I called him about the lion.

Layne decided to no longer hunt lion for himself, and now acts only as a professional guide for others interested in hunting. He has participated in the capture of 50 (when I shot mine) to probably 75 lions by now. My friends, Juan and Rocky Lopez (brothers), and Juan's son, Juanito, have all shot lions under Layne's direction.

And then there's the story about the one who got away. We spotted a big, beautiful lion up in the rocks, probably bigger than the lion I shot. He was fast and far away. The dogs couldn't get to him, and we couldn't get a shot. But then, my great joy was always in the ride, climbing those mountains to "no man's land" and looking out the great expanse of beauty. There is no experience like that, and I will always be grateful to Layne for giving me that opportunity on so many occasions.

Bob Cheever (age 15) with big moose (Wyoming)

Bob Cheever's big male lion (Arizona)

The NRA and ILA

I have been a member of the NRA for a long time. I have been a life member since 1986. My son, Allen, is a junior life member. For Christmas I get memberships for family members and friends. I keep several NRA applications in my briefcase at all times. Whenever the opportunity arises, I solicit a new member. I believe all gun owners and sportsmen in the U.S. should be members and support this fine organization. They do a good job fighting for our 2nd Amendment rights. They also do a good job of trying to educate the citizens and elected officials of this country.

I, for one, would like to see this country educate children in public schools about gun safety and the need for law-abiding citizens to be able to defend and protect themselves and their families. I believe our country is 180° off-course when elected officials try to pass more gun laws. We need more law-abiding citizens owning guns and trained to use them. It doesn't take a rocket scientist to figure out that guns don't kill people, people kill people. We should have strict laws (and we do have) on the books to severely punish individuals who use a firearm to rob, kill, or maim an innocent victim. Then we need to stop the entire plea bargaining and watering down the crime and put the lawbreaker behind bars. Double the sentence when a gun is used and no early releases. This country has gotten soft on crime. This needs to change.

Ollie Barney, George Parker, and Harlon Carter were responsible for the formation of the ILA (Institute for Legislation Action). The ILA has done a good job of fighting for our 2nd Amendment rights in Washington. I, like most of my friends, regularly contribute to this organization.

The NRA frequently sends mail to me, asking me to write my elected representatives urging them to vote one way or another on a particular piece of legislation. I always do, and I hope millions of others do. All of us interested in owning guns in this country need to take an active role in preserving our rights. Join the NRA, donate to the ILA, write your representatives, and vote for the candidate who is pro-gun. And spread the word. The NRA needs all of the help that they can get.

I have always lived in a rural area of the United States. It is very important to me to own a gun. I am not going to rely on the 9-1-1 telephone operator to protect me or my family.

Happy Trails...
Layne Brandt

About the Author

Layne was born in 1944 to Otto and Sophia Brandt. He is the oldest of 3 children. We have a younger sister, Karen Hoback of Amado, Arizona.

We were raised in a rural area, near Holland, Michigan, on a 40-acre family farm. We raised strawberries, raspberries and blackberries and fattened a few steers every summer. We always had a lot of animals...dogs, horses, rabbits, birds, pet raccoons, etc. Us kids always had lots of chores to do. The 1st job that Layne and I can remember was growing pine tree seedlings. Irrigation and weed control were very critical. At the end of the 3rd year, Dad sold the small Christmas trees. He deducted his expenses and split the proceeds between Layne and I. We learned at an early age the value of a dollar and hard work.

Dad had an old M-20 Farmall tractor with a hand crank. It was a trick to start and harder to drive. We had to level land with Dad on the Fresno, plow snow, and any other job that needed to be done. Layne and I were driving the tractor and his pickup by age 9.

When Layne turned 10 years old, mom and dad gave him a .22 single shot rifle and a .410 single shot shotgun. That was a real step up from the old Daisey BB gun. We were allowed to hunt on the farm and some of the neighboring farms. We had 2 neighbors close to Layne's age, Larry Breuker and Glenn Vande Vusse. They enjoyed hunting as much as we did. We hunted sparrows, starlings, rabbits, crows and pheasants. Whenever our chores were done, we would go hunting.

We attended a one-room school about ½ miles from our house. Glenn Vande Vusse and Layne were the only two kids in their class. We had one teacher for eight grades. She would give everyone their daily assignments and then go read her book. If anyone misbehaved, she promptly swatted us with her ruler. For all practical purposes, we had to educate ourselves.

After high school, Layne joined the U.S. Army. He endured basic training in Ft. Leonard Wood, MO. Later he spent 6 months in Aberdeen, MD, where he graduated from a mechanics' school. He spent 3 years in active duty and was discharged a Specialist 4th Class. He qualified expert with the M-1 rifle and the carbine rifle.

After the Army, Layne moved to Laramie, WY where he continued to pursue his love of hunting. He spent several years in Wyoming and met several lifelong friends. He enjoys visiting Wyoming every chance he gets.

He moved to Sahuarita, AZ in 1969. He currently manages 5600 acres of pecan orchards owned by Farmers Investment Co. (FICO), the largest pecan farm in the world. He earned his pilot's license in 1977 and has logged over 3500 hours in the company Cessna 182.

Layne has also been very active in the pecan industry. He has served on the Board of Directors of the Arizona Pecan Growers' Association and the Western Pecan Growers' Association. He has also served as a grower delegate on the National Pecan Marketing Board.

He has also been very active in gun related issues. He has taught 4-H Hunter Safety Courses and has served on the Board of Directors of the Arizona Chapter of the Safari Club International. He strongly supports the NRA (National Rifle Association) and the ILA (Institute for Legislative Action). He believes every gun owner in the United States should be a member of the NRA.

In the mid 1980-s Layne became acquainted with Ollie Barney, who taught him the techniques of hunting mountain lions with hounds. Layne became very interested in the sport. Ollie has caught over 200 lions so far and Layne has caught over 70.

Layne lives in Continental, AZ with his wife, Eileen, and their son, Allen. He has 4 daughters: Kelly Haskins of Portland, OR; Tamara Aidlin of Seattle, WA; Lisa Brandt of Oakland, CA; and Julie Rayner of Green Valley, AZ.

I hope you enjoy reading this book as much as I have enjoyed hunting with my brother.

Dale Brandt, Rio Rico, AZ

**Layne Brandt
with FICO's Cessna 182
Sahuarita, AZ 2000**